FROM THE
WHEELHOUSE

Tugboaters Tell Their Own Stories

Other Books by Doreen Armitage

Around the Sound: A History of Howe Sound—Whistler

Burrard Inlet: A History

FROM THE
WHEELHOUSE

Tugboaters Tell Their Own Stories

By Doreen Armitage

HARBOUR PUBLISHING

Harbour Publishing Co. Ltd.
P.O. Box 219, Madeira Park, BC V0N 2H0, Canada
www.harbourpublishing.com

Cover design by Roger Handling
Page design by Warren Clark
Cover photo by Don MacPherson
Half title photo of Captain Vic Di Castri, c. 1975 on his tug *Brunette*, built in 1890, courtesy UBC Library Rare Books and Special Collections, MacMillan Bloedel Ltd.
Printed and bound in Canada

Harbour Publishing acknowledges financial support from the Government of Canada through the Book Publishing Industry Development Program and the Canada Council for the Arts, and from the Province of British Columbia through the BC Arts Council and the Book Publishing Tax Credit.

Library and Archives Canada Cataloguing in Publication

Armitage, Doreen, 1931-
    From the wheelhouse : tugboaters tell their own stories / by Doreen Armitage.

Includes index.
ISBN 1-55017-293-X

    1. Tugboats--British Columbia--History. 2. Towboats--British Columbia--History.
3. Ship captains--British Columbia--Biography. I. Title.

VK139.A75 2003   387.2'32'09711
C2003-911082-6

To my own favourite crew…

Jessie, Scotty, Andy and Kelly,

with love

Acknowledgements

My deep appreciation goes to the tugboaters whose stories make up this book. I have developed a strong admiration for their ability to work under stressful conditions and coolly handle emergencies. Their familiarity with BC's dangerous waters and unpredictable weather is justifiably legendary. Had Rudyard Kipling not already used the title, I might have called this book *Captains Courageous*. During interviews, when I expressed amazement at problems tugboaters had overcome, the men's common response was a humble, "But that was my job. That's what I did."

Thank you, gentlemen.
Doreen Armitage

Note: Every effort has been made to use accurate geographical names. In cases where accepted or vernacular usage varies from the proper name—where a skipper has referred to Tattenham Shoal (properly Tattenham Ledge) or Schooner Pass (properly Schooner Channel) or Hecate Straits (properly Hecate Strait), for example—the terms used are those of the skippers.

Key to photograph sources: LB: Captain Larry Baese; CMC: Council of Marine Carriers; VPL: Vancouver Public Library; DM: Captain Don MacPherson; VMM: Vancouver Maritime Museum; CVA: City of Vancouver Archives

Contents

Introduction

The following are reminiscences of disaster, boredom, wild winds, practical jokes, breakaway barges, relentless tides and camaraderie. As one retired skipper says, "Towboating can go from humdrum to nerve-racking, but all in all it's a dandy job."

Towboaters work in small vessels—the wheelhouses in some tugs are no bigger than closets—yet they deal with the most powerful elements. Their work is dictated by currents, wind and tides, and by the flood and ebb in the straits, on the outside coast and up the Fraser River. In BC, their territory spans the province's 27,000 kilometres (16,800 miles) of coastline and includes rugged islands, bays and desolate inlets. And British Columbia-based tugs venture north to Alaska and south to Washington, Oregon and California.

The earliest tugs were usually wooden-hulled, side- or sternwheelers powered by wood-fired steam. The first steam tug on the coast, the

In the early 1900s the *Lorne* was one of the most powerful tugs on the coast and often towed large flat booms. Flat booms were, and still are, used in tows but most booms consist of bundles—each bundle containing the same volume of wood as a logging truck, or more. HARBOUR PUBLISHING PHOTO

Beaver, burned from seven to nine cords of wood daily and was reportedly so underpowered that it couldn't buck a current and blow its whistle at the same time. To feed the *Beaver*'s voracious appetite, crew spent days ashore chopping and sawing or lugging cordwood aboard. At least one old paddlewheel tug pulled a barge heaped with firewood to heat its boilers and when winds were favourable, hoisted a sail. Other early wooden work boats on the coast included such sturdies as the *Isabel*, the *Maggie*, the *Alexander*, the *Otter*, the *Pilot* and the *Etta White*. They linked the coast as part of the so-called lifeline (along with the Canadian Pacific's Princess ships and those of the Union Steamships) and were eagerly awaited by isolated settlers and loggers. The shrill of a tug's whistle in a fog-clad inlet cheered more than one gyppo logger.

Beginning in the 1880s, wood-fired steam engines gave way to more efficient coal burners. Coal required less bunker space than wood and, after the coal docks at Departure Bay and elsewhere opened, it was easily obtained. But coal was filthy and the interiors of coal burning tugs were coated in black dust. Diesel oil began to replace coal in the 1920s. Then, in the decade before World War II, roaring diesel engines began to power more tugs. By 1950 about 35 steam tugs were all that was left of a once great fleet of BC steam tugs; of those, perhaps three were coal-fired. In the 1960s, steel hull construction gradually replaced wood. Several thousand tugs in all have worked the coast, lakes and rivers—each with its own character.

While early tugs towed sailing ships into port, the main work of later tugs was towing logs. The earliest log tows were made up of logs cabled together in any of several designs. The cigar-shaped Davis raft, 46 to 61 metres (150 to 200 feet) long, was formed from a woven base of chains, cables and logs, with loose logs wired down on the top. Each of these massive rafts contained about one million board feet. Flat booms were, and still are, used in tows but most booms consist of bundles—each bundle containing the same volume of wood as a logging truck, or more. In open-water areas of the coast, wood had to be transported by barge. The earliest barges were hulls of old sailing ships, filled with cargo and often towed by paddlewheel tugs. Over the years the fleet of large, rectangular, straight-sided barges have been joined by self-loading, self-dumping and self-propelled log-carrying hybrids.

Versatile BC tugs and their equally versatile crews have towed just about everything—food, machinery, rocks, gravel, wood chips, hog fuel, paper, oil, salt, lumber, salvaged vessels, oil rigs, railway cars, dredges, fish scows, deep-sea ships, even houses. If it can be towed, chances are a BC tugboater has put a line on it.

CHAPTER 1

All Fired Up for Steam

Whether tall men found a tug's cramped quarters too uncomfortable to remain in the industry, or small men made better—"cattier" was the term—deckhands, neither Captain Larry Baese nor anyone else seems to know. But Captain Baese, like many towboaters, is a compact man. And he shares with many veteran skippers another characteristic: a thoughtful soft-spokenness. Recalling his working days from his Langley home, Captain Baese, now in his seventies, is measured and calm. The same characteristics served him well during five decades on West Coast tugs.

Plumes of black smoke were a familiar sight in the days of the steam engine, and large crews were needed to run the machinery. The *S.D. Brooks* had two oilers, two engineers and two firemen. VMM

Captain Baese is old enough to have caught the tail end of the steam tug era. His first job, in 1946, was aboard the Coyle No. 3, *a stalwart steam tug in Pacific Coyle Navigation's fleet. During the early 1950s, when many towboat companies operated on the Fraser River, he worked as a deckhand for Burt and Reid Towing, Stradiotti Brothers and others. In 1975, some 26 years after receiving his master's ticket, Captain Baese purchased the 65-foot tug* R.B. Green *and joined the relatively select cadre of tug owner/operators. With his son working as crewman, Captain Baese towed logs out of Lake Bay, Hole in the Wall, Seymour, Toba and Bute inlets. Captain Baese retired in 1990.*

The SS *Beaver* ca.1888. The first steam tug on the coast, the *Beaver* burned from seven to nine cords of wood daily and was reportedly so underpowered that it couldn't buck a current and blow its whistle at the same time. To feed the *Beaver*'s voracious appetite, crew spent days ashore chopping, sawing and lugging cordwood aboard. CVA

On the steam tugs we used to burn coal and we'd go into Union Bay [Vancouver Island] on the way north and load up. My job as deckhand on the mate's watch was to run the coal chutes. About five Chinese

fellows would come down the dock, never speak to anyone except each other, and they'd go into the hold. One of them yelled when they were ready. I'd pull on a rope on the coal chute and a bunch of coal would come shooting down into the hold of the boat. Then he'd holler and I'd stop and they levelled the load. He'd holler again for more coal until the hold was packed. Halfway through they would come out, black with coal dust. They'd come into the galley and put five spoonfuls of sugar into each cup of tea. I guess that's where they got their energy. Then they'd go back down into the hold. That was a terrible job. We'd get the coal packed in then head north. There was coal dust all over the boat.

On my watch I'd go up to the wheelhouse with Sammy, the mate, and stay there until about 2:30 a.m. when I'd go down and put the coffee on. I had to bunker up the stove in the galley because it was also coal. That was the deckhand's job, to keep the stove going all night and also empty the ashes. Sammy would go down about three o'clock for his coffee and I would take the wheel, and when he came back up he'd send me back to make sure the hot water was on for the cook, who got up at four.

The firemen had to start cleaning up the ashes from the coal in the engine room about 3 a.m. They'd pull all the ashes out onto the steel floor then shovel them into a five-gallon bucket. I would be up on deck to work the crank inside of the funnel. The fireman put this five-gallon can inside the funnel and I'd crank it to the top and take it out and dump it in the ocean. Then I'd crank it down to the engine room and we'd keep this up until all the ashes were cleaned up. By then I was full of coal dust, too. And there were no showers. You'd get one set of linen—two sheets and one pillowcase—for the entire trip. If you were out for 30 or 40 days that was it. You brought your own towel. There was no change of blanket. You had to use the blanket that was on your bunk for maybe many months.

Getting rid of the ashes was pretty well the end of the watch for me. I'd steer for about a half-hour and Sammy would tell me to go down and wake the cook. This cook was an alcoholic, as a lot of tugboat guys were in those days. He was the nicest guy, name of Scottie. He had cases of beer under his bunk and hard stuff. I'd wake him up and while he was lying in bed he'd pop the top on a beer and drink that whole thing. Then he'd get up, shake, and say, "Aahh, the nectar of the gods." Then he'd go into the galley and he'd open another beer, take a bottle out of the cupboard, take a shot of rye, wash that down with a bottle of beer, then say, "Okay, now we can go to work."

Capt. Donald MacPherson restored this old telegraph in use in the 1920s. The pedestal on this one is steel, but usually it was made of brass. DM

One night we were coming out of Ladysmith, running light. Sammy was the type of guy that could remember all the courses in his head. I hardly ever saw him look at a chart. I was at the wheel and he gave me the course and I swung the tug around until we were on course. Steam tugs are so quiet you can hear anything out of the ordinary. I knew something was different, so I looked down and the water was full of fluorescence. The whole bow lit up. Sammy reached back and took the handle of the telegraph and put it full astern. I didn't know what he was doing. He switched on the searchlights and they lit up the sky like you wouldn't believe. We were in a bay. He'd given me the wrong course. He'd realized, after thinking about it for a few minutes, that he'd made a mistake.

Mention the name Stanley to a group of veteran towboaters and at least one is bound to say, "You must mean Alan!" Captain Alan Stanley and his brother, Peter, are well regarded in the maritime community for their knowledge of the coast. Both men worked on the water for many years and both eventually became BC Coast Pilots. Captain Stanley, who is of First Nations descent, lives in North Vancouver. Now retired, he and wife Dawn often travel the province in their camper. He, too, is soft-spoken and genial.

Capt. Alan Stanley

Captain Stanley spent his childhood on Quadra Island and from age 10 fished with his father at Rivers Inlet. At 13, on his summer holidays, he worked as second engineer on the Harris No. 8 of Pacific Coyle Navigation and saw first-hand the miserable conditions firemen and coal passers worked in. By age 15 he was working as a deckhand on Coyle Towing's Peerless. In 1948 he became deckhand on the Norshore and continued as mate until 1952 when he moved to Vancouver Tugboat Company. He received his master's certificate in 1955; the La Rose was his first command. On the La Rose and other tugs he towed chip, hog fuel, and gravel scows from Vancouver to Howe Sound, Vancouver Island and

elsewhere. Captain Stanley stayed with Van Tug until he became a BC Coast Pilot in 1967. He retired in 1997.

One time we were up at Gowlland Harbour and we started a new coal passer. Passers shovelled the coal out of the hold to the boilers so the firemen could fire up the boilers to keep steam up to generate power. The fellow didn't care for the job so he left us in the middle of the night and Captain Gordon Davis wanted me to be coal passer because I was the youngest on board. So I did that for three days until I got back to Vancouver. I had to get down inside the tug beside the boiler and shovel the coal into the bunkers. It was difficult because there wasn't much room between the boilers and the inner skin of the tug. When I would turn around to get a shovelful of coal and then turn back to pass it down, I'd be banging my knuckles. I got quite dirty, too.

Steam tugs *Sea Swell* and *Norvan* tied to a log boom. The *Norvan* was previously the North Vancouver Ferry No 1.
J. HENDERSON COLLECTION, PHOTO W. LOCH.

When we got to Vancouver we hired a new coal passer. I stayed on the tug as deckhand until school started. One of my jobs was to take the ashes that the firemen raked out of the fires and dump them over the side.

We had 10 men on board. In those days we needed a large crew because everything required so much work. Even though we didn't have radar, the steam tug was much easier to navigate than a diesel tug because of the quietness. When you wanted to verify your position, you'd blow the whistle and count and on the steam tug you could easily hear the echo from shore. On a diesel tug the noise made it harder to hear the echo and get an accurate position.

At Vancouver Tug I had the opportunity to be master on a steam tug in the late 1950s. That was really interesting. Van Tug had taken over another company and in their holdings they had an oil-burning steam tug, the *Sea Swell*. That was a nice job. All the other tugs I had been on as master were diesel. This was my only opportunity as master on a steam tug. One of the ways that a steam tug differs from a diesel tug is in the manoeuvring. When you wanted to go from ahead to astern it was so quiet you couldn't tell if your direction had changed. Sometimes you had to look at your wash to see if you really were going astern whereas on a diesel tug you could tell immediately from the sound.

Captain Joe Quilty's career in towboating is as diverse as the decades his career spanned. From the time he stepped aboard Island Tug & Barge's Salvage Queen in 1934, until he retired from the Department of Fisheries in 1982, he worked as deckboy, deckhand, mate and master on many tugs. He's seen foul weather and dangerous situations—in fact, he is likely the only West Coast towboater to have willingly steered his craft in front of anti-ship guns during a firing exercise. This was during World War II, when he was skipper on the target-towing tug General Lake. Now in his eighties, Captain Quilty lives in a pleasant home overlooking a golf course in Ladysmith. He is slim in build and circumspect by nature. To listen to him talk of his time on tugs is to get a sense of eras past and of great experience.

I started as a deckboy for my board on the steam tug *Salvage Queen*. She had been the *Tees*, a CPR coastal passenger boat. When we were out on the west coast about 1935, we were heading for Nootka Sound to pick up a Davis raft. We were fighting a westerly all the way up the west coast. I was so seasick. I was in my bunk in the fo'c'sle and the portholes were leaking, so every time she dipped under a sea the water would pour in and was sloshing all over the fo'c'sle floor. There was a steam radiator in the middle and every time the water would hit the radiator the smell of hot seawater was horrible. The mate, Jack Gillam, came down and he said, "You'd better get up. I think we're going to sink." I said, "I hope we do!" I really meant it. I was just a kid. He picked me up out of my bunk and carried me up on deck and laid me down beside the funnel where it was warm. That was quite a day. We didn't sink but she was a pretty old ship and was taking quite a beating out there, popping rivets and leaking. There was no such thing as seasick pills in those days. Navy scientists in World War II developed them, I understand. Later on I finally got over being seasick.

We were towing barges of hog fuel from Chemainus to Port Angeles, Washington and then from Port Alberni to Ocean Falls and Port Alice and returning with empty barges. In those days the barges were actually hulks of old sailing ships with their masts and decking removed, the whole hull an open hatch and boarded up about 10 feet above the hull both sides and fore and aft.

On the *Salvage Queen*'s last trip in December 1936, we were towing the empty barge *Island Gatherer* from Ocean Falls. I was on the *Gatherer* with Captain Poulson and his wife. The two of them lived in

The *SS Salvage Queen* shown here on May 17, 1933, was so badly damaged when involved in rescuing crew from a barge in December 1936, that she had to be retired. PHOTO BY WALTER E. FROST

the barge's aftercabin that remained from the sailing ship days. The bargees and Captain Poulson were responsible for dealing with the towing lines, steering behind the tug and firing up the steam donkey that was used for anchoring. We ran into a hurricane in Queen Charlotte Sound, a very rough stretch of water. We found out later that the winds were reaching about 80 miles per hour that night and the crew on the *Queen* was having a lot of trouble with the tow line. The brake was continually slipping, allowing the line to slowly work off its drum. When the crank disks on the winch snapped in half from the

pressure, the brake couldn't hold the line back and it ran off the drum. The four of us on the barge were cut off from the tug, and the wind was wild. We lost sight of the boat and figured that was the end of us. But we knew that our skipper, Fred MacFarlane, had promised that he would never abandon his men on a barge that had broken loose.

He somehow found us again, got close, and the other bargee jumped off the barge onto the tug but Mrs. Poulson (who was very seasick), her husband and I were left. Captain MacFarlane was finally able to get the tug in position, close enough that we could throw Mrs.

The Mosquito fleet, including the *Etta White* July 15, 1913, BC. Early wooden work boats on the Coast also included such stalwarts as the *Isabel*, the *Maggie*, the *Alexander*, the *Otter* and the *Pilot*. They linked the Coast as part of the so-called lifeline and were eagerly awaited by isolated settlers and loggers. CVA

Poulson onto the tug's foredeck where the crew caught her in a canvas tarp. We then were able to leap onto the tug's deck without injury, although the tug took a lot of pounding from the barge, causing a great deal of damage. It was really a miracle no one was lost or injured, but the *Salvage Queen* was damaged beyond repair. The wheelhouse was crushed, the hull holed and the davits snapped. After that I moved onto the *Snohomish*, a former US Coast Guard vessel, which Island Tug purchased to replace the *Salvage Queen*.

If all the working and retired towboaters who live in North Vancouver ever formed a political party they could take over city hall. North Vancouver is widely assumed to have the largest population of past and present towboaters of any community in BC. The explanation for their great numbers is simple: not only is the area close to work for those employed by Burrard Inlet-based towing outfits but it also offers a fine view of the active harbour.

Captain Alan Wood lives in a well-tended North Vancouver home. Soft-voiced, he has a serious demeanor that fails to mask a lively sense of humour. Many of his stories are accompanied with a chuckle or smile. Captain Wood's first job on the water, in 1945, was as a dishwasher on the Union Steamship Camosun. He later deckhanded on the tugs Chilliwack and Island King of the Frank Waterhouse Company and the RFM of Marpole Towing. He also worked on the Master which has been restored by the SS Master Society. Captain Wood retired in 1995.

Capt. Alan Wood at the wheel of the *Cates IV*, ca. 1981. ALAN WOOD COLLECTION

Steam tugs could not carry very much water so the tanks would have to be replenished approximately halfway down from Seymour Inlet to Howe Sound. One way we filled up was to tie our boom of logs against the beach at Green Point Rapids, where there was a big waterfall. Then I climbed up the rocks with a sea anchor, attached the fire hoses to the bottom end of the sea anchor, attached it to a rock and put it under the waterfall. It would take me about an hour to fill the tanks, then I'd take the whole

procedure down, untie the boom and carry on. As you got farther down the coast there were more communities. We'd stop in at Lund or Stillwater or Pender Harbour and get water from a tap. On the *Sea Lion*, if we were desperate for fresh water, we'd take advantage of a heavy rain by setting up hoses under the drain on the top deck and let the rainwater run into the tanks.

When I look back, I realize that we didn't wash ourselves that often, even though we had lots of hot water on the steam tugs. On the *Sea Swell* we had a full-sized bathtub but we didn't have showers on those tugs. We used to have sponge baths instead, a couple of times a week. We had a great way of washing our clothes. We'd partly fill a bucket with water, add soap and our dirty clothes. Then we'd attach a

The *Sea Swell* was one of few remaining oil-burning steam tugs in the 1950s. Unlike diesel, steam tugs were so quiet skippers would often be unable to distinguish when they had changed directions from forward to reverse. VMM

toilet plunger to a piston as tall as I am and set the bucket under it. It worked like a washing machine. Then we tied a rope around the bundle of clothes and threw the whole thing over the side to rinse in the prop wash.

In Captain Howie Keast's *North Vancouver home there is a humble-looking album containing photos and clippings of a remarkable life on the water. He has been awarded the Canadian Star of Courage medal and the Humane Society of BC Award. A spirited man with a genuine and easy smile, Captain Keast is reticent to talk about his personal life but quick with stories about the men and tugs he worked with from the 1940s to the*

Once queen of the BC towboat fleet, the *Sea Lion* was restored and modified for charter work after 60 years in service. VMM

1980s. Captain Keast was 17 when he went to work at C.H. Cates & Sons Limited in 1939. He worked for Escott Towing on Burrard Inlet for several years before joining Lyttle Brothers (later North Arm Transportation), where he remained for 30 years.

They didn't have the luxuries of today's tugs, but being steam, they were quite warm and comfortable and the food was good. However, the tugs of today with diesel engines are far superior in accommodations and big horsepower in comparison to the *Massett* and the *Moresby* in their day. They could tow only up to 56 sections of logs with seven to nine crew members, whereas a diesel tug, lesser in size but with more

In those days, when vessels came into First Narrows past Stanley Park they were required to blow a whistle because there was no radio contact. If you were towing a log boom or barge you would blow one long whistle and two shorts to tell any vessels outbound or inbound that you were coming into the Narrows. Other vessels had to blow one long whistle. I remember the old steam tug *Sea Lion* coming into First Narrows blowing its whistle in the tune of "How dry I am, how dry I am, I am so dry."

Captain Howie Keast

Canadian government steamer *Newington* was a BC lighthouse tender before becoming a tug. Capt. Larry Baese was on the *Newington* when it ran aground just before the Christmas of 1950. CVA

horsepower and a smaller crew, can tow 60 sections of bundles. The old steam tugs entering the Yuculta Rapids couldn't buck their tows up to Dent Island because of the currents. They would have to take the long way round, along Sonora Island then out into the back eddy that would carry them into Mermaid Bay to wait the next tide. The diesel tugs could pull right up to Dent Island and have to wait for a short time if they were too early for the tide into Mermaid Bay.

Captain Larry Baese: In December 1950, we left our tow tied up at Secret Cove. We thought that once Christmas was over we'd go back and get it, then we could get home for New Year's. But we went up and back so quickly that the dispatcher told us to go back and pick up a tow at Port Neville. So with long faces, we headed north. We had to go into Pender Harbour to get some groceries at Irvines Landing and water for our steam tug, the *Newington*. It was a 135-foot boat with a crew of nine men. Just before midnight it was time to leave because the skipper wanted to hit the rapids at the right time. He came out of Pender Harbour and headed north. He was going to go up between Nares Rock and Pearson Island. But with no beacon on the rock at that time he cut too soon and hit Nares Rock at full speed. It was pretty close to high water and there was no way we were going to come off because he had just rung full speed, and she did about 11 knots running light. I remember I was coming out of my cabin when I heard the bow wash starting to break, because on a steam tug you can hear everything. She hit and we took quite a lurch. Of course the boilers were all fired up for steam and if you don't use that steam it could blow. The engineer was concerned because with the boat leaning so far over to starboard, he didn't know what would happen. The tug kept leaning further and further and the crew was all standing on the high side. The lifeboats were impossible to get off. So I suggested to the skipper that I should go up to the wheelhouse and blow off some of the steam through the whistle. The skipper didn't want anyone inside in case anything happened, so he had me go up on top of the wheelhouse where I pulled on the whistle cord.

We could see all the house lights come on, including their Christmas lights. It was quite a show. Of course they could see us out there because we had our lights on. A fleet of boats came out to give us a hand. Our fireman and a deckhand got on one boat and they went into the hotel at Irvines Landing and got a hotel room and charged it to the company. The rest of us were taken to Boom Bay on three Pacific Coyle tugs—the *Faultless*, *John Davidson* and *Coyle No. 1*. Then the *Coyle No. 1* went back to our tug because they didn't know if someone would put a line on her and claim salvage. Four of us went back with her and stayed all night. I went on board to make sure all the doors and vents were closed because when the tide came up, if the water could get inside, she wouldn't rise. As soon as the tide rose she righted herself no trouble. She had a double hull and we kept fresh water in between the hulls. She didn't leak but salt water got in there. We discovered this when we got up to Port Neville, so we had to turn

In a reminiscence published in *The Westcoast Mariner* magazine in May 1989, one old-timer recalled the "compound chorus" of the steam tugs' well-oiled voices. The triple expansion engine on the *Marmion*, he said, whispered "swagglety slish, swagglety slish" from its crossheads and piston rods, the "grumpity ha, grumpity ho" of the vacuum pump, and an additional "pooh cha" dropped in here and there. He owned one engine that mumbled "tapockata fump, tapockata fump." He remembers the Gardner engines as having a darkly coloured "rumblety pah, mumblety po," which he enjoyed as a comforting rhythm.

around and go back to Vancouver. We had a 24-gallon water tank for emergency and that provided the steam to take us home. By the time we got to Vancouver there was hardly a drop of water left. We didn't make it for New Year's Eve but we were home for New Year's Day and a good dinner.

John Henderson's stories of West Coast towboating are unique for several reasons. As an engineer whose working life was spent among valves and pistons, he came to know tugs in ways that were completely different than skippers. And as someone with a lifelong interest in tugs, he has an amazingly broad knowledge of the craft and the men who worked on them. Show John Henderson a grainy old snapshot of a West Coast tug and chances are he will be able to tell you the name, the era and the tug's history.

John lives in a house in Victoria with his dog, Dennis. By his own admission he is "no good at talking," so he wrote out his stories. It was one of the delights of researching this book to receive an envelope from Victoria and open it to reveal pages of John's tiny, neat handwriting. His stories are highly informative and include the kind of thoughtful detail that only someone who feels deeply about West Coast tugs could note.

John Henderson's uncles owned MacFarlane Brothers Towing Limited; as a child in Victoria he used to go out on the company's steam tugs. He started as a deckhand on the Masset *in the early 1930s, served in the*

The *Moresby*, June 6, 1926. Though quiet and cozy, steam tugs could only tow up to 56 sections of logs with seven to nine crewmembers. Today's diesel tugs, lesser in size but with more horsepower and a smaller crew, can tow 60 sections of bundles. VMM

VE 006 A SNOHOMISH

Canadian Navy, then worked on a number of steam tugs before becoming an engineer on cruise ships.

The powerful steam tug *Snohomish* of the Island Tug and Barge fleet was built on the east coast of the United States in 1908. CMC

So far as the steam tugs went, they always shone like they were solid silver or gold. Handrails shone. Brass and other brightwork shone. Engines had canvas tops with edges frayed out with Turk's head knots finishing them off—simply beautiful to behold.

When I was on the steam tug *Moresby*, the deck plates in the engine room were enamelled bright red. They were diamond plates, rolled when they were milled and had raised diamonds on the surface. After covering them with a thin coat of paint, we rubbed them with sand or emery paper so the diamonds shone. The effect was that they looked just great and we were proud of them. So was the chief. I remember he came down to the engine room about six one morning, looked around and said, "He hasn't wiped the deck." There was a bit of cigarette ash on it. I told him that the fireman had been having trouble with the fuel and had been late getting around to his usual end-of-the-watch clean up. "Okay," he said. "Don't let it happen again."

On the steam tugs we used to have oilers whose job was to oil the machinery. On the *S.D. Brooks* we had two oilers who did just that, two engineers and two firemen. The old up-and-down engines had a lot of oil holes that had to be oiled regularly. In those days they set watches as soon as they left the dock and stayed watchkeeping until they returned to Vancouver or wherever. The watchkeeping was on a

two-watch system and the chief engineer was on from six to 12, the second from 12 to six, the skipper from six to 12 and the mate from 12 to six.

It's a funny thing, but when I was on the tugs there was not a great lot of funning around. We did what was required of us. On the other

Steam tug *Haro* in its coal-fired days, ca. 1913. It became the *Le Beau* in 1957. VMM

Years ago the Chinese cook at the hotel at Port Renfrew befriended a brown bear. The bear would come bumming around the kitchen and the cook would feed him. This went on A-okay for awhile with the bear getting more aggressive and finally, literally, taking over the kitchen. The cook had to complain to the hotelier, who decided that the bear had to go. He got his rifle and dispatched the bear to eternity. There were a couple of tugs laying at the wharf and the chief of one tug was a practical joker. He got a couple of hands and they dragged the bear down to the other tug and put him into the chief's bunk, pulling a blanket over him. Later on the old chief was going to turn in for a nap. He was a bit of a windy person and went into orbit, shouting "Bear! Bear!" The rest of the gang gathered and found the dead bear, all of them laughing fit to burst at the chief's dilemma.

The Port Renfrew beer parlour was a pretty wild place in those days. A wild fight erupted, so the hotelier closed it up. The usual tug was laying at the wharf, so the crew dragged the tow line up the wharf, around the hotel, and shackled it together. They then threatened to pull the whole issue into the sea if the beer joint did not reopen. The poor owner complied.

John Henderson

hand, there was unpleasantness from time to time. A guy I know up in Ladysmith was telling me that when the deep-sea tug *Snohomish* came to the Canadian Registry she was a coal burner. She had been in the US Coast Guard for umpteen years and one of the compartments on her was labelled "Brig" and had been used as a temporary jail cell. One young fellow on the *Snohomish* was a trimmer, keeping the coal levelled. This kid decided that he wasn't going to shovel coal any more. The chief took him up to the skipper, who had been an officer in the Royal Navy during World War I. They'd cooked this plan up. When the kid stepped into the skipper's cabin, the old man was sitting there with a revolver on his desk and he was polishing the shells. So he looks at the kid and says, "Oh, you're giving us trouble, are you? You're not going to work any more?" The kid says, "That's right." "Well," the skipper says to the chief, "get the mate to take him down and lock him up in the brig. We'll give him a little bit of naval discipline."

One of the Powell River tugs was dieselized during the 1930s. The company was hot to remove the oiler because he wouldn't be needed with the upgrade. They had two engineers and one oiler. The chief told them to give him 24 hours notice if they decided to remove the oiler. Well, this morning the tug arrived in Vancouver with the paper scows. The manager was down and met the chief who was in his go-ashore clothes and had his go-ashore bag in his hand. The manager, who was a pretty nice guy, asked the chief what was the trouble. The chief answered, "Don't you recall what I told you when you started talking about taking the oiler off? I said if the oiler goes I'll paint the engine room black. Go and have a look at it. I'm gone." And he was. I heard of him years later. He was doing okay, had a service station and automobile agency out on the King George Highway in Surrey municipality.

Another set-to involved Big George, a deckhand, and Jimmy Zamit, the cook on one of the tugs where I was working. They got bitching at one another at breakfast time. I can't think what the kafuffle was about but when I got out on deck they were there. George had a rifle and Jimmy had a big butcher knife out of the galley. They were threatening one another. Probably George was saying something like, "Put that effing knife down or I'll shoot you, you SOB," and Zamit was saying, "I'll cut your heart out if you don't put the gun away." Then the door of the skipper's room opened and the big skipper came out, wearing only his seaman's jersey, tee-shirt and jockeys. He was swearing, never repeating any profanity even once. The mess boy said later, "I learned some new swear words off the skipper today, and he is a quiet man!" So the skipper threatened to can them both. At that point the cook interjected, "It's okay, Captain. I'll quit, George can stay." So that's the way it ended and the skipper shouted for the wireless operator to phone Vancouver for a cook as the effing cook had quit.

There is another yarn about the chief engineer and the skipper who used to booze it up together. One day they sailed out of Vancouver during late afternoon. The skipper joined the chief for a smash before dinner. After a bit, the chief went out on deck to relieve himself and the tug gave a little roll, tipping the poor man over the gunwale. Minutes later the old man [skipper] was looking for him and concluded he must have fallen overboard. He turned the tug around and went back and spotted the chief splashing away and picked him up, inviting him aboard for a drink—of his own booze.

One time we had M.R. Cliff, the owner, aboard the *Haro* and we ran down to Lund one day for water and a beer. At the last minute, M.R., in a fit of generosity, decided to buy a couple of boxes of beer. At any rate, the guy at the hotel asked if he wanted to pay cash or charge it up as spuds or some such. Then the shit hit the fan. M.R. Cliff was not pleased and he was going to can the lot of us. Anyhow, we were on the way back to pick up the tow and I was sitting on a box on the fantail aft and the old fellow came along and started to growl about charging beer up as spuds. Some guys used to charge it up as milk. That would not have happened at Cliff's. We never drank fresh milk there, only at Kingcome and some of the high-class outfits but we could get only a two-day supply because we didn't have refrigerators.

I don't know how to advise you about language on all the boats. It seemed to be universally bad, but if people who read books want to read it like it is, I have to be honest. When I was chief engineer of the *Wm. J. Stewart* it was the funniest thing. I would go on board and within five to 10 minutes be roaring and blaspheming like the rest of them. A terrible habit. This Captain Delaney was a Liverpool Irishman. They were usually pretty rough but "effing bastards" was usual language for him. I remember one cook he got rid of for incompetence who went to work on the *S.D. Brooks* in 1949 when I was there. As one humorist on board so succinctly stated after he'd tasted the cooking: "That effing bastard Billy couldn't parboil shit for a tramp on a fine day!"

CHAPTER 2

Life Aboard

Captain Royal Maynard has worked on tugs for over three decades and he knows life aboard is unpredictable. "I've seen times when we were supposed to be out for two days and the trip lasted over 20. Not too many years ago I was going out for one week on the *Escort Protector* and that trip turned into 54 days. I never got off the boat once. When you pack to go to work you don't pack for the length of the trip. You pack for what the length of that trip might be—anything up to two months."

Seen through the wheelhouse windows of the *Seaspan Discovery*, an enormous bulk carrier transports its load of coal from the Port of Vancouver. DM

Captain Maynard lives in a pleasant home in Madeira Park, Pender Harbour. Now 60, he is old enough to have worked with many of the great steam-era skippers yet young enough to have observed more recent trends in the industry. He remains active as a skipper on the 6,140-horsepower Rivtow Capt. Bob.

One of Captain Maynard's closest personal connections was with towboater and search and rescue pioneer, Captain Cyril Andrews (whose stories are included in this book). Until Captain Andrews passed away, in May 2003, he and Captain Maynard talked by phone every day, no matter where Captain Maynard might be. Captain Andrews called Captain Maynard "son"; they had a great respect for each other.

Captain Maynard started on tugs in 1960 and within six years had his master's ticket. He has been with Rivtow Marine for 35 years. His work has taken him from Washington State to Alaska.

Years ago a tug left Vancouver and went up to Smith Inlet just above Cape Caution for a tow of logs. Now up there they had flat booms but they were what they called Oregon dog booms. They had wires running across each tier of logs, lag-bolted into the logs to hold them, and around the outside. Where the normal boom had only boomsticks, these would have master wires on them. It took quite a while to get one of these tows together. The boat and tow were ready to go in about two weeks but the weather was no good. The crews on that boat worked a month on and a month off. When the original crew's month was up, they ran to Port Hardy and changed crew there by plane. The relief crew came up and they sat with that same tow for a month, ran to Port Hardy, changed crews back to the original crew, and they sat there for two weeks longer on that tow before they moved it. Weather has always been a big factor in towing logs.

When I first started on the boats in 1960 most of the tugs were towing 20 to 30 sections of flat booms. I've had lots of people say that there's not much moving in the way of logs on the coast any more. You only see one-quarter or less as many boats out there towing logs. What they don't realize is that each boat is towing more than what 20 boats would have towed 40 years ago. Each tow is all bundles and much bigger. The volume of wood that it is moving is a lot more than it appears to be.

Captain Alan Wood, *who described earlier the innovative ways steam-era towboaters washed clothes, recalls that log towers, especially, faced long delays:*

After the tow was made up in Seymour Inlet, if the weather was bad sometimes we had to wait a week, two weeks or even three weeks for the swell out in Queen Charlotte Sound to go down. When you're tied up that long there really isn't that much to do and it can get very boring. You can paint out your room four times, paint the bathroom again, or paint anything you looked at to keep busy. Sometimes the garbage piled up on the boom alongside the tug, so you moved the tug

A distance that would take 24 hours travelling light, could take weeks towing a boom. The very slow speed made the trip a little boring at times and deckhands' days were occupied washing, painting and polishing brass. The skipper and mate were primarily occupied with navigation. DM

down the boom a bit and started on a fresh pile of garbage. While we were towing logs as well, the weather was very important. Coming down the coast, if the water got really rough the steam tugs used to pump oil over the side to break the waves so they didn't crest, they'd just be a long, easy roll. It wouldn't happen today. That saved some of the logs from coming out. Years ago that was standard practice. You

used to get down to Sechelt, and the last run of the trip was always the longest because Sechelt and Howe Sound had no protection. That part of the coast was always a hang-up.

What do tugboat crews do while they're towing a log boom? Heading up the coast to get a tow of logs we used to go to a place called Seymour Inlet, halfway across Queen Charlotte Sound on the main-

Launched in 1982, the 6,140-horsepower *Rivtow Capt. Bob* took over as the most powerful BC tug. Capt. Royal Maynard skippers this famed tug. VMM

The tug *Standfast* tows a barge loaded with timber. VMM

Opposite: The tug *Le Beau* tows a woodchip barge bound for a pulp mill. Previously the steam tug *Haro*, it was purchased by Vancouver Tugboat in 1957 and renamed. DM

land. It used to take us 24 hours to run up there light and 30 or 31 days to come back with a tow. Mainly you have to watch the weather so closely and you're not moving very fast. The deckhands' days are occupied washing, painting, polishing brass—they wouldn't have much problem filling their days. But if you were the skipper or the mate you spent your whole day steering the boat, which did get kind of boring. You have to spend your whole time watching the weather because the boom of logs couldn't stand any weather. That was the skipper's main concern. Otherwise there wasn't much to do. Coming down the coast you're looking at the same land for hours on end. You can't seem to catch up with what you're looking at and you don't pass where you are very quickly. After you came into Vancouver you'd get 24 hours off then go out and do the same thing again. The speed for towing logs was one and a half or two knots, so tides played a big part in your travels. If you had a big head tide you didn't go very fast, if at all. You might just sit and look at the same point of land a long time.

You used to travel close to the beach; we called that beachcombing where the boom of logs is only 20 or 30 feet off the beach. The tide wasn't supposed to be as strong near the beach so you dragged the boom as close to the shore as you dared. That kept you occupied.

One particular trip we were going up to Squamish on Howe Sound to pick up two lumber barges, drop one off at Woodfibre and pick up an empty barge to come to Vancouver. This picking up of the barges was all off my watch. I'd been up all day, had had only an hour or so of sleep and had to be up again for another couple of hours, so by the time we finished and were heading back to town I was very tired. As soon as we got the tow line out I went to bed. The next thing I heard was a horrendous crash, a lot of noise and a big bump. I leaped out of bed and opened the wheelhouse door to find nobody in the wheel- house, the windows steamed up, and I had no idea where we were. I opened the door on the starboard side and saw the Defence Islands. We were right across from them at Brunswick Point. The mate told me that he'd fallen asleep shortly after we left Woodfibre. It turned out that the barges behind us never caught up to us so that wasn't a problem, but we were worried about damaging the hull. When we backed the boat off the beach there was no water leaking in so we carried on and delivered our barges.

The *Seaspan Commodore* tows a self-loading/dumping log barge to Port Moody at the eastern end of Burrard Inlet. To unload, the barge's tipping tanks fill on one side with seawater, causing the barge to tip and dump the logs. DM

I used to dread going in the North Arm of the Fraser River because when you were going down the river with two big chip barges, the tide ahead of you, especially at night, and you were confronted with five or six big log tows all spread out across the river in front of you, it looked like you were going into a city. You didn't have any idea which side to pass on, whether to go down the middle or down the sides, so communication with these tugs was vital because they told you as best they could which side to pass them on and hopefully it turned out all right. Going upriver, the other way, with a 7,000-ton load of rock 25 or 30 feet behind you and a flood tide, the same thing, only you're catching up to the log tows and there's no way to stop, and you're confronted with the same problem—which side to go on—so it becomes very stressful. I was glad to get out of there.

One retired skipper, *who prefers to remain anonymous, remembers that Port Renfrew on Vancouver Island was often weatherbound:*

They used to bring the small booms out from Nitinat Lake. They'd nip them down to Port Renfrew to a log tie-up there, then a tug from Victoria, the *Anna Gore,* or whatever, would wait weather with 20 or 30 sections or so and lay up alongside the boom and wait until the

weather moderated outside Port Renfrew enough to give them time to get the thing down to Becher Bay before the weather turned. I've laid out there for as much as two weeks. You'd go out at every turn of the tide, have a look, nope, come back and tie up to the boom and go up to the beer parlour. In the old days you could wait as long as a month. You always put the gear on in readiness. Once you've hooked up to the boom, which is quite an operation to get all the heavy gear onto it, and once you're outside the harbour, you're committed. You can't turn back because now the current is up your back and you're goin' like hell. And there is no shelter for the next six or eight hours. You've got to find a window in the weather and it's up to the skipper to decide. He's always having to forecast. If it goes wrong the boom starts to disintegrate and you've got a million dollars' worth of logs floating around.

Earlier I was towing log barges for Island Tug on the SS *Sudbury*. I was dayman deckhand. The log barges are so heavy—they're so many

Once a navy corvette, the *Sudbury* was converted to a deep-sea salvage tug in the 1950s. Extensively overhauled for salvage operations, the 193-foot long, 2,750 horsepower *Sudbury* became famous for its dramatic rescues. CMC

hundreds or a thousand times heavier than the tugs. That means the tug is really on the edge of control some of the time. And you can't get near the barges—the logs stick out on each side like porcupine quills. If they take a run on you and swerve sharply, you have to be careful you don't get sucked alongside on a short tow line—say at Camp Point or Seymour Narrows. They're very difficult things to handle because of their weight. Large tugs, as large as they get, are nothing compared to the weight of these things. If the barge decides to take charge, there's not a helluva lot the tug can do except eventually, over time, straighten it out. Even with the biggest tug, the *Rivtow Capt. Bob* or the *Sudbury II*, it's like putting an outboard on the end of a ferry.

There are big cranes on log barges and they'll load up in just a few hours. We'd take them south to Squamish or wherever, then the little assist boats, boom boats, came alongside the tug and took usually the mate and one crewman off the tug, put 'em on board the barge, and

Vancouver Tug's first self-dumping log barge in Sooke Inlet sliding out from under a load as its tipping tanks fill with water. DM

they'd go down below and open the valves to flood the tipping tanks. We used to go aboard, go below, open the valves and close the hatches, and then get inside one of the pylons (log stops at the end of the barge) or we could get thrown right off. As this thing heels further and further over, the tipping tanks on one side flood. Then suddenly, if it works properly, the barge actually pops out from under. The logs don't slide off, the barge pops out. So you have to slacken off the tow line on the tug in a helluva hurry or it's going to pull the tug over. Somebody once rode on top of one of the crane towers and pretty near broke his neck. He was so high, it was like whiplash. He never rode the tower again. He was one of the white hats on shore—one of the people that walk around the dockyard looking important—superintendents, administrators. Nowadays most of the bigger barges may be radio-controlled and the skipper can stand on the tug and push a button to operate the valves. It's under full control. They also self-discharge. Crewmen don't even have to board them.

The log barge tugs only unhook every two or three weeks when they change crews and come back in for fuel. They hook up in

Vancouver, go up, load, come back, dump load, don't unhook. They're on a very short tow line when they're dumping and the skipper has to be tending the winch brakes because when the barge pops out from under the load of logs it can smash up a large tug pretty badly. The log barge will scoot sideways up to a hundred feet, and if you're on a short tow line it pulls the tug along like a rag doll and will pull it over. Actually they smashed up one tug. The skipper didn't let the brake go and they had the tow line really, really short, so when the barge took off they couldn't release the brake and they had the whole back end of the tug under water. Smashed the winch. The cook was on deck and he was thrown in the water. He went so far down he couldn't see any daylight. He popped his eardrums. He estimated that he was about 60 feet under. They pulled him out but he never sailed again. Surprisingly few people ever get hurt because of their familiarity with the routines. It's dangerous work, it's extremely dangerous at times. With the bigger tugs and the bigger barges, the weights and forces involved are so heavy and the barge always outweighs the tug. Towboating is a very specialized business. You can sink a boat or kill people very, very quickly. You always keep your eyes open.

Captain Howie Keast, *who spoke of the "how-dry-I-am" tune of the* Sea Lion's *whistle, recalls the work-and-wait of log towing:*

With Point Grey Towing we used to go down to the jetty, at the lower part of Point Grey on the North Arm of the Fraser River. We made up

Opposite: Built in California in 1943, the *Sudbury II* had a decompression chamber on board for divers and a well-equipped machine shop for making spare parts. VMM

The *Sea Lion* in 1905, the year it was launched in Vancouver, BC. Respected for its towing power, the *Sea Lion*'s original three burner Scotch Marine boiler was converted to oil after WWI and its tall funnel reduced by more than six feet. CVA

long tows to go up the river on the flood tides. They would be made up of anything from 30 to 40 sections. There would be two to four tugs on those tows, depending on the tide, and they were taken up under the bridges, maybe dropping some off along the way, then up to the top end and into the main river where they were delivered to various mills. It used to take sometimes two tides, but in the spring, when the freshet was on, it was hard going. The tides used to run so hard they would only slacken up a little at the high water at New Westminster, which would be three hours after high water at Point Atkinson.

In bygone days when the tugs took tows down through the Yuculta Rapids, they used to go into Mermaid Bay to wait tide. Usually, if they hadn't been in there before, they would make up a wooden plaque, put the name of the tug and the date on the plaque and nail it to a tree in the vicinity of the tie-up spot. Of course

A regal 130-foot *Sea Lion* after it was modernized and outfitted with an 800-horsepower Enterprise diesel engine.
HARBOUR PUBLISHING PHOTO

everyone that came in would look at the new ones that had come up. To my knowledge, when I was in there, every tree on the shoreline was taken up with the names of the tugs. Some of them had been up there for so long that they were slowly deteriorating and the names were hard to make out.

The towboat strike of 1970 caused many changes in the industry—the design of new tugs being built, two radars on board, sleeping quarters above deck and many other things. One was a regulation regarding hours of rest for the crews. This situation had been a real problem for a long time. Often, with a two-man crew on a small tug, it was impossible for either man to get his full six hours of rest if this shift coincided with a duty, like picking up a barge, for instance. As a result the crew could be working 24 hours with no sleep, a dangerous situation. With the new, rigidly enforced hours of rest regulation, the skipper, mate and crewmen were required to complete their six hours off duty, no matter what else was happening, or they would be fined $500. The whole idea was good, but in an emergency the skipper, in reality, could not refuse to come to the wheelhouse. I only knew of one instance when the skipper broke the rule because of a severe situation. Later the regulation was softened a little.

*Captain **Ron Westmoreland***'s *memories of West Coast towboating are as clear as the view of Vancouver harbour from his North Vancouver apartment. Like many retired towboaters, he remains intensely interested in tugs but he has the added big-picture perspective of a man who worked dispatch for many years, co-ordinating tugs and jobs.*

Capt. Ron Westmoreland, 1992.

Opposite: Time to reflect: crew take a break aboard the old steamboat *Charles H. Cates IX,* built in Vancouver in 1912 as the *Moonlight* and later sold to C.H. Cates and Sons and renamed. VMM

Captain Westmoreland received his master's ticket in 1957 and ran L & K Lumber's tug, the Jean L. *In 1965 he came ashore to work dispatch and remained in that position for 26 years.*

In 1945, at the age of 17, I left high school to work full-time at Cates. At that time our work week was 12 hours a day, six days a week if work was there, if not we'd get off early. And for that we were paid $44.50 a month. Anything after six at night or before six in the morning was

Adorned with rope bumpers, the bow of the 63-ton harbour tug *Charles H. Cates IX*, ca. 1920. VMM

overtime. After we had been there a while our salary was slowly increased to $79.50 a month, which was top wages for deckhands at that time. It doesn't sound like much but I ran a Ford Model A on that. It's all relative, though. The car only cost $150 to purchase, gas was 25 cents a gallon. It's just about the same nowadays if you figure it out. I worked on all the Cates tugs from time to time, including the old steamboat *Charles H. Cates IX*, previously the *Moonlight*.

In days gone by there was no radar, all navigation was done by compass. In the late 1940s we were on a harbour trip. I wasn't too knowledgeable and we were heading up to go through Second Narrows. I was freeing up some shackles on the stern deck. Skipper was steering and blowing the whistle, trying to get echoes from shore because we were in thick fog. That was the way we navigated, but mainly with the compass. He called me in to steer while he stuck his head out the window for a while to listen for echoes. I had a big pipe wrench in my hand so I just wrapped a rag around it and set it on the bunk, inches from the compass. The next thing, instead of going through Second Narrows, we were right alongside a grain elevator in Vancouver. He couldn't figure out what had gone wrong. It suddenly dawned on me that the wrench had dragged the compass around. I would pretty near have got thrown overboard if he had known. While he wasn't looking I picked up the wrench and took it outside. I guess he chalked it up to some mistake in navigation. I sure learned a lesson there.

Another thing I learned early on was that tapping the barometer was a no-no; only the skipper could do that. You couldn't play around with that stuff at all. This was before radar so you depended a lot on

While waiting for the tug's next assignment, a crewman of the *Seaspan Guardian* changes the bulb on the anchor light at Roberts Bank. DM

your compass and radio and barometer and whatever aids you could muster. It was strictly up to the skipper to handle that equipment. You shouldn't tap the barometer, just leave it to the skipper because he would tap it every so often, whenever he decided, maybe every three or four hours. It would move slightly, one way or the other, each time he tapped it. He wanted no one but him to tap it so he could tell if it was rising or falling. If people came in and tapped the barometer every time they passed it he wouldn't know what it was doing, going up or down.

When it got near to Christmas the companies attempted to get every crew home for the holiday. The crews would tie up their tows and leave for Vancouver. If, on the way, they met a tug with a tow they would assist by tying up alongside it. Sometimes as many as six tugs were assisting as the tow came into Burrard Inlet. They all had Christmas trees on their masts.

When I started on the tugs, for quite a few years the tradition was for everyone to have a Christmas tree up on the mast. There were many log-towing tugs around and in foul weather they would tie up to a bluff or wherever they could in sheltered waters and they would go ashore with an axe, find a nice little tree, chop it down and put it on the mast. At Christmastime everybody had one. Log towing has changed where it's mostly done by barge now, and they don't often tie up for weather reasons. The tradition is still carried on by some. Cates, I understand, buys a few small trees, puts them in the parking lot and lets the guys help themselves, which my son does every year. My youngest son goes out and buys a tree for his tug to carry on the tradition, which I appreciate, and puts it on his mast. There's still a fair amount of it I suppose, it's just done a little differently.

The logs we towed were called pee-wees, small gang saw logs. You could hardly walk on some of them. They were so small that we had gear, dog lines, attached to big spikes driven into each log with a chain through them, and we'd run that across the head and the tail end of the tow and if the wind started to blow, the logs would bounce. If they bounced out they were still fastened together so you wouldn't lose them. Without the dog lines, once one log bounced over the tail stick it would go down and the rest of the logs just floated out. So we used to use gear like that. I used it all the time when I was towing outside [of the harbour]. It was an ounce of prevention, that's all. It was a lot of work to put them on. Some of the logs were so small we carried planks to walk on because the logs wouldn't hold us. Then eventually they went to bundle booms. They bundled 10 or 12 logs together and that eliminated the need for a lot of this.

A tradition still carried on by some, towboaters tied Christmas trees to the mast to show the holiday spirit. Captain Charlie Cates, one of C.H. Cates three sons and former mayor of North Vancouver, peers through the wheelhouse window. VMM

Probably the worst experience I had, the one that really upset me, was late one night during 1960. We were running light on the *Jean L.*, crossing the gulf, heading for Victoria through Active Pass. There was a pretty strong northeast blowing. I was getting a couple of winks of sleep and my mate woke me and said, "We're floating pretty low in the water." So I got up and took a look and saw that the stern deck was

under water. So I went down below and the engine room had a good foot of water above the deck plates, and the water was pouring in through the hatch. We had a three-inch pump aboard, a good big one that worked off the main engine. I engaged that and went back up and got the mate working on the deck pump, loosened off the lifeboat just in case, and I called Captain Cyril Andrews at Search and Rescue to see

Tugs and fish boats, including *Pacific Monarch*, *Earl*, *Moresby*, and many others at the Gore Ave. wharf in Vancouver, July 22, 1926. VMM

if there were any boats in the area that could stand by in case things didn't work out. There was one of the CPR boats in the area and he was going to heave-to until we were okay. The big pump took care of it and afterwards I found out that the hatch, although fastened, hadn't sealed properly. We made it into Active Pass and had a new alternator and starter sent over the next day. We flushed the engine and reduction gear to remove any salt water. A tug called the *Standfast* was in there. He sent his engineer over and he gave me a hand to do all these things. It was very much appreciated. There was real camaraderie on the boats then. The night before, however, some newspaper reporter had been listening in on my calls and phoned my house. My wife was about eight months pregnant and he told her that I was sinking and had called for Search and Rescue and how many kids did I have. It really shook her up. And when I got home and my wife told me, I was so upset. I found out who it was and phoned his boss and did the same thing to him. I told him I wasn't sure but I thought his wife was in an accident out on the street, I thought a car hit her. He got all upset and I said, "I'm only kidding you." He started to yell and curse at me and I explained the whole situation to him and told him he could go and tear a strip off his reporter because that's not good reporting. He assured me he would and that was the end of that. I don't have any use for reporters because of this.

The 118-foot iron-hulled *Newington* built in Scotland in 1912 at dock in Vancouver, September, 1955. VMM

Captain Larry Baese, *who was on the steam tug* Newington *when it ran aground just before Christmas of 1950, recalls how he got started in the business:*

My first job was working on the docks. They were converting the *Pacific Monarch* from a coal burner to an oil burner and my job was to haul

scrap metal off the tug and sort it into different piles on the dock. I think the reason they hired me was that I was bugging them every day for a month for a job and this was their way of getting rid of me. Then they put me out decking on the *Coyle No. 3* with Len Davis, who later changed his name to Don Davidson when he went to work for Great West Towing. He was a great guy, the only guy I ever sailed with who, as an adult, would sit down and read the funny papers and laugh like hell. He hurt his back and got off the boats and Captain Norman F. Beazley came aboard. He was like a father to me, the greatest person. If I did something wrong like coming down to the boat, 15 years old, drunk, he took me in the wheelhouse and backhanded me all around because he didn't agree with guys coming on the boat drunk. I never

Log-towing tug *R.B. Green* in Bute Inlet tied to a bundle boom, 1991. In 1975, some 21 years after receiving his master's ticket, Captain Baese purchased the 65-foot tug and joined the relatively select cadre of tug owner/operators. LB

did that again. He wanted things done his way. At the beginning of a trip he'd be after me to do things the way he wanted. By the time we got back, I was feeling good about what I was doing and would go back out with him again. I worked with Norm for four and a half years, and in that period was only decking about eight or nine months. At that time you couldn't get experienced mates with everybody just coming home from the war. He'd have to stay up with the mate because a lot of times they were inexperienced. The only time he got any sleep was when I was on his watch. So finally he went into the office and told them that if he had to rely on me to get his sleep, I might as well take the mate's job. So I was promoted to a mate at the age of 15.

Then I was decking on the *Faultless*. That was an experience because Sammy Nicholson was the mate and he had been in a fire at one time. His ears were burnt off and his face was really disfigured. He was the greatest guy. At first I was scared of him because you'd look at this face and he would give you a mean look. The first day he asked the two deckhands what watch we wanted to be on. The other guy's name was Mike King and he said, "Oh, I want to go on the skipper's watch. I was the first on board so I get the first choice." Sammy looked at him with this mean look on his face and said, "You'll go on whatever watch I tell you you're going on." He backed off from Sammy; he was so scared. I was afraid to say which watch I wanted to go on after that. So I just said, "I'll go on your watch, Sammy." That was the best move I ever made because he was so good.

*It has been more than 50 years since **Captain Aage Fransvaag** sailed into Burrard Inlet on a deep-sea freighter but his talk is still flavoured with a pleasant Norwegian accent. Buster, as he is universally known in the towboating community, is both fast-talking and quick-witted. Recalling that first trip to BC, he says he looked down from the deck of his freighter at the little tugs and thought: only dumb Canadians would work with such small tugs. But he married a Canadian and settled in Vancouver. By the mid-1960s he was working for Gulf of Georgia Towing Company as deckhand, then became a skipper with Vancouver Tugboat Company. Captain Fransvaag's stories are from the years before he became a captain:*

[The cook] brings harmony to the crew because he knows what kind of food they like—steaks rare, eggs sunny side up. If he's a competent baker, so much the better, making bread, rolls, buns. How they come into that class of being a traveller's cook, I don't know. Experience? On

Le Roi's crew enjoying freshly harvested butter clams in Espinosa Inlet, Vancouver Island, ca. 1961. Note the excellent condiment-laden lazy susan suspended over the galley table. DM

the other hand you can have some cooks that you can't get to co-oper-
ate. They become snarly, then the crew gets snarly, and it just doesn't
work. One cook used to make cake doughnuts, oozing with beautiful
lard, some of them rolled in sugar. Then he made beautiful cream
puffs. There wasn't a skipper, mate or deckhand that could tell these
cooks how to do it. On the smaller tugs we had mate/cooks, deck-
hand/cooks. Once I was told to cook a pot roast. I didn't even know
what it was. It was so bad that the engineer told me that if I ever went
in the galley again the company would fire me. That was my last experience with cooking.

The food supplied by the company was staples, they called it. It

was just that. The cook bought extras. I remember a cook that came to me and asked me the first time, "How would you like some steak?" I said, "What do you mean steak? In Norway we only get steak once a year on Christmas Eve." He said, "T-bone steak or club steak?" I didn't know what the heck he was talking about. So he asked, "Would you like it with onions?" "Sure," I said. Then he said "Would you like mushrooms?" In Norway we don't eat mushrooms. They're *champignons* and imported from France. "Sure, give me everything," I said. And I think the whole crew sat there watching me eating my very first towboat steak. Wow!

Esther, one of the first lady cooks, came aboard. She was a born

Named after the company's founder, the 136-foot *Harold A. Jones* was the flagship of Vancouver Tugboat's fleet. Two 1,750-horsepower engines provided its impressive power. DM

Two superstitions are common on tugs. Don't open a can of milk upside down; it could cause the boat to turn over. If you do, throw the can overboard immediately. Some crews tear the labels off the cans so they can't tell which way is up. And never whistle in the wheelhouse or you'll whistle up a storm. Some crews believe in less common superstitions: don't leave port on a Friday; don't shave on board or the wind blows; always put your left shoe on first. In the old days, if a seagull landed on the bow, you wouldn't chase it off and wouldn't let the captain catch you if you did. He would tell you that this was an old friend that had come to visit from the hereafter.

Of course, the time-honoured belief that women are bad luck on a boat is now scoffed at, but Captain Alan Wood shares a story about the possibility of that old superstition influencing a trip:

One day I took a visiting female friend of the family out on the tug while I was going into English Bay to pick up a pilot from a ship. As he was coming down the rope ladder, something happened to the long ropes supporting the ladder and its lower edge rose up in a loop. The pilot was halfway down and was tipped upside down. He hung there with his coat flapping in the wind. Very seriously, the lady turned to me and said, "Does he always come down that way?"

cook. She had grown up on her dad's fish boat and was used to men's environment. We had a difficult time figuring out what toilet and shower facilities she could use because they didn't have too much choice on the *Harold A. Jones*. She always went ashore with two or three crew members. Never by herself. She used to say, "Don't worry boys. I won't come and rape you all." We had her for two or three trips. At that time it was an experiment to have a female cook. Now, I understand, they have quite a few.

As was common practice with most towboaters, we used to pull tricks on other tugs. Up in the river we would set a carton of eggs in the sunshine so that they would rot. Then we threw them at the other tugs in the dark. Stealing tie-up lines was another trick we used to pull. Island Tug had different colour lines from Vancouver Tug. So we kept stealing from each other's barges. It became a game. We had piles of ropes—this pile was Vancouver Tug's and that was Island Tug's.

Captain Royal Maynard, *skipper of the* Rivtow Capt. Bob, *recalls the unique initiations facing inexperienced crewmen:*

A typical tugboat trick is to send the new guys to get green oil for the green light or red oil for the red light. One time we tied up the tow over at Paul Island near Lasqueti. One deckhand was young and green. He knew he liked oysters but he didn't know where they came from. There was a good oyster bed up by the end of the tow where it was tied to the beach and there was a good tide about one o'clock in the morning for getting oysters. It was blowing a gale, southeast, and raining and not too far above freezing. The mate and I put him up to making an oyster trap—building a runway out of rocks. Then we told him that right at low water he had to stand at the water's edge, or right in the water, and bang pots and pans to drive the oysters up into this trap he'd made. While he was out banging pots and pans together, the mate and I went over to the other side of the point and picked up a bunch of oysters and put our two full pails on the deck. When the deckhand came back, there were his oysters. I don't think he ever forgave us for sending him out in the pouring rain, wind and cold for the better part of the evening even though it was only meant as a joke.

You see and hear of lots of comical things happening on the tugs. I recall one time a tug had dropped its tow of logs, just let it go, and dropped into Refuge Cove to get fuel and groceries. Old Norm who had the store there years ago, used to have a little booze around the place and didn't mind sharing it. While the crew was gone, another tug

A Cates tug assists two other Seaspan International tugs move a huge self-loading log barge in Burrard Inlet's busy harbour. J. HAYES PHOTO

from the same company figured out what was going on, picked up the tow and took it around the corner and tied it up to a bluff. When the crew finally got back out, it took them quite a while to find their tow.

When I first started on the boats I was pretty hard to wake up, probably because I hadn't matured yet. I remember being wakened up by a bucket of cold water in my face and at the same time a boom chain landing on the steel deck above my head. Rather a tough way to wake up but it tends to make one think twice before sleeping through a call again.

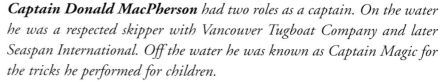

Captain Donald MacPherson had two roles as a captain. On the water he was a respected skipper with Vancouver Tugboat Company and later Seaspan International. Off the water he was known as Captain Magic for the tricks he performed for children.

Captain MacPherson has been retired for 10 years but his extraordinary brown eyes light up when he recalls his days as a deckhand on Vancouver Tug's the La Dene, *towing logs from* Bella Coola *to* Ocean Falls, *or as a skipper in the 1950s on the* La Mite, *setting up tows on the Fraser River for outside tugs.*

Mate Donald MacPherson at the wheel of *Le Roi* in 1961. Just visible right of centre is the telegraph and at right foreground is the binnacle that houses the tug's compass. DM

Most chief engineers on the outside tugs took great pride in their boat. The engine rooms were kept so clean you could eat off the floor. Every nut on the machinery was polished, as was the cast iron engine bed and the steel railings. Actually the rails were not only polished to a shine but sanded in the opposite direction, sideways, every six to 10 inches or so to form a pattern. The engineer was continually painting the engine itself and the rest of the room. Pipes were painted different colours to indicate what was running through them—fresh water, fuel, lube oil, etc. Another engineer coming aboard would know immediately what each pipe contained as the colours were the same for all of the tugs.

The skipper would signal to the engine room with the telegraph, a circle of metal with speeds marked on it and a lever to indicate the desired command. For instance, if the skipper signalled "Slow Ahead" a bell would ring in the engine room to get the engineer's attention, and he, in turn, would adjust his telegraph in response, which would ring a bell in the wheelhouse to signal the skipper that his order was carried out. Nearly all the outside tugs in the '50s and '60s also had bells and jingles aft—a large gong [bell] with a smaller bell [jingle], side by side, for the skipper to use when he was yarding logs from the stern, to pass on orders to the engineer. For example, a jingle before one bell indicated slow ahead, and slow astern was a jingle before two bells. They also had voice pipes to let the skipper talk to the engineer from the wheelhouse. This arrangement was the source of many practical jokes. If the engineer had his ear to the pipe the captain might pour some of his tea down. The engineer would later reciprocate by calling for the captain over the pipe then shooting flour up through it with an air hose.

The engineers proudly kept their working areas immaculate. The floor of the *Seaspan Venture*'s engine room was shiny checker-plate, and the railing was polished into a pattern. ca. 1980s DM

Chief Engineer Carl Ryan inspects the engine room controls on *La Pointe*. All metal surfaces shone and the area was spotless. ca. 1959. DM

We were towing for Vancouver Tug on the Fraser River, but Rivtow, Straits Towing, Point Grey Towing and others had tugs working there, too. Our tugs were medium sized, about 65 feet long with 600 horsepower. We took barges loaded with woodchips or hog fuel [sawmill bark and junk] down the river from as far away as Mission to the tie-ups off Point Grey where the outside tugs would come, drop off their empty barges, pick up the loaded barges and take them to the pulp mills. Then we'd take the empties back up the river, two or three at a time, and drop them at different mills. On our tugs there were only two crew members aboard and it was dangerous for the deckhand doing the tie-up because the skipper couldn't see him when he was at the opposite side of the barge and wouldn't know if the tug was holding the barges in the right location for him to attach the lines. We didn't have radio communication then to keep in touch with each other. When he was done he would come back to where I could see him and would have to use hand signals to let me know what was happening, like crossing his wrists to show me that the line was attached.

To get to the mouth of the North Arm from Mission we had to go through five swing spans—the old railway bridge at New Westminster, the Annacis Island bridge, the Fraser Avenue bridge, the Twigg Island bridge and the BC Hydro bridge immediately west of Oak Street. That was the toughest one because it was on an angle. We had trouble with that many times. We were pulling a 50-foot-wide barge through a hole 60 feet wide. It was always risky. At freshet time when the water level was at least 16 feet on the Mission gauge, we were required by law to turn the barge around above the bridge and drop it through the hole backwards. We had to have another tug there pushing against the back of the barge so it could go through very gently. Bridge Towing did the assist work there. They would sit at the bridge for 24 hours a day to assist tows into the bridge opening. When the river was running normally we didn't need an assist. Some skippers heading down the river would put out five cigarettes on the console, almost as a joke, one for each bridge. They called them "Bridge Pills." The situation could be very tense because if we weren't really careful we could tear out the bridge.

We were always very careful to ensure that our compass was accurate. We would check it in clear weather and go right around the compass rose. It was called swinging your compass. You didn't want to find out in fog that you were 20 degrees out.

One of our skippers liked to play jokes on the crew members, like putting eggs into their gumboots. Some of the eggs weren't too fresh.

Don MacPherson held his first tug job on the *La Dene*, owned by Vancouver Tug and Barge, here moored at Ocean Falls, ca. 1952. The tug was 105 feet long, with a 400-horsepower Atlas Imperial engine. DM

One time, when I was on the *La Dene*, an outside tug, there were all kinds of seagulls around. When the skipper went off watch the mate and I put a string out on the deck with a loop at the end and some bait in it. Then he'd pull the loop tight when a gull landed in it and catch it by its feet. It didn't hurt them. They didn't even flap their wings. He caught several, then pushed the porthole to the head open and stuffed the gulls inside, where they were very quiet. There were seven or eight in there when the skipper opened the door. They all wanted out at once. He just about went over the side. We had lots of jokes played. My engineer would throw a few eggs at the operator of the old Marpole Bridge when he was out on the swingspan. He couldn't go anywhere. He would have a carton of milk sitting out in the sun and to get back at us he'd drop the whole carton on the tug. Another time the *La Dene* was heading to Marpole to change crews and passed the *La Fille* pulling a tow. The skipper on the *La Fille* was helpless to manoeuvre but as the *La Dene* went by, the crew pegged eggs at him. After we had tied up at the dock, and the *La Fille* had tied up her tow, the *La Dene*'s skipper was in the head having a shower. The *La Fille* came up to the same porthole as the seagulls had been pushed through and put his hose into the head. When our skipper opened the head's door to escape, his clothes floated out ahead of him as he charged out soaking wet.

Captain A.E. (Ted) King *knows about the kind of jokes Captain MacPherson was involved in because he was a deckhand on some of Captain MacPherson's tugs. An energetic man, Captain King lives on an acreage in Langley, surrounded by fields dotted with peacefully grazing sheep. Since 1989 he has worked as a Fraser River pilot but he has been around the water all his life. At age 16 he purchased a commercial fish boat and fished the Fraser River and Rivers Inlet. In the early 1960s he went to work for Vancouver Tugboat Company and became a master in 1969. His first command was the* La Bette.

La Fille tows the historic steam tug the *Master* into a temporary moorage at False Creek. The *Master*, built in 1922, was retired in 1959, but purchased by the World Ship Society and acquired by the SS Master Society ca. 1960. DM

We used to do a lot of funny things. Mind you, I think we were a different group of people in those days. Everybody was gung-ho. There was no slack time. There was a place to work and a place to joke. Most of the time it was work. Everybody was pushing everything. The tugs and barges were getting bigger and we were towing more all the time. When the *Le Prince* came out we thought, my gosh, here's a tug that's got an engine as big as one of our deep-sea tugs that used to run down to California. It was 600 horsepower. Holy mackerel! As tall as I was.

Tug engines became more powerful as the tows grew. The *Le Prince*'s 600-horsepower Stork engine was among the largest and loudest for boats of its size. DM

A great big Stork engine down there just a-thundering. Everybody knew us on the river because of its noise level, especially at freshet time, when you'd be coming down the river and looking over the dikes at the farms. You'd just hear this engine going boom, boom, boom, boom.

In a more serious vein, on the *Le Prince* we used to make runs up to Port Mellon and Squamish and back. We were the first ones to ever tow five empty chip barges. We used to take a second deckhand but the skipper always told him to stay out of our way because we knew exactly what we were doing. We went up there one night and they just said to bring the empty barges home. So we just coupled up all the empties and started out with five barges behind us. We came around Point Atkinson and the office called and asked what barges we had and we started giving the dispatcher numbers. He said to do that again. Then he said, "There's five of them?" It was still dark and other tugs called us wondering what the long thing was coming around Point Atkinson that they had picked up on their radar. So the dispatcher told us we were moving along pretty good and to drop two off at Kits buoy and take the rest of them to the river. Everybody couldn't believe that. And we were even a half-hour early to go home.

I heard about one captain, a retired pilot now, who would come aboard every morning and have his cuppa tea. The crew would sit and chat with him, then he'd go down and use the head. They knew that. So he went down to the fo'c'sle and started to yell these terrible words, and what kind of animals worked on board this boat, the head was just disgusting. So the other skipper went down to the fo'c'sle and looked at the toilet and says, "Oh my gosh, this looks like somebody's privy. They've made a mess of the toilet bowl." He puts his hand in the toilet and scoops up some of the mess and licks his hand. He says, "There's nothing really wrong with that you know." Well, the other guy ran upstairs and threw up over the wall. They'd scrubbed the toilet out perfectly clean and put peanut butter down all over it.

If asked, Harbour Cruises' skipper Captain Robert (Bob) McCoy will augment the standard Burrard Inlet tourist commentary that he delivers to passengers with information that only a veteran towboater could know. He'll point out where the tug docks used to be and describe the bundle boom—in other words, he'll tell them the working history of the harbour.

Most weekends Captain McCoy leaves his Saanich home to run tour boats for Harbour Cruises in Burrard Inlet. He enjoys the work and says it is a way of staying connected to the waterfront where, in 1944, he got his first job aboard. That was as deckboy on the Princess Alice. *He worked on local tugs as oiler and deckhand, went deep-sea, then in the early 1960s returned to BC. Over the years he worked for Canadian Tugboat Company, Coast Ferries, Vancouver Tugboat Company, Northland Navigation, Gulf of Georgia Towing Company and Seaspan International. He retired from tugs in 1995.*

You look at any tugboat and it looks like someone has gone crazy on them with a hammer. They're all dents and gouges. This is all from barges caught in the wind or working the tide and current because it's quite tricky at times. I used to stand on the stern at Duncan Bay sometimes and just watch in amazement what was going on with the barges.

There were four [conference] calls per day, at 8 a.m., 11 a.m., 4 p.m. and 10 p.m. with all the fleet that was out. I don't think they bother with that any more. They've got telephone contact to the office now. The office kept track of each tug, primarily for the customers they were servicing, so they could tell them that their equipment, or whatever, would be in at a certain time. We'd tell them what weather we were having so they'd know how we were progressing. This happened on the outside of the island as well as the inside.

Captain Alan Stanley

Barges were running this way and that way. Dolphins got broken, pilings got broken. We have a damage file on every tug. You have to report every accident no matter how slight. I remember reading in one skipper's logbook a report about when he was towing two barges along near Hardwicke Island. He wrote, "I couldn't believe my eyes." Evidently the back barge took off in the back eddy and came right around the island and ran between the first barge and the tug. It put a kink in the tow line at the bridle link but it didn't even hit the tug or other barge.

If there is a story about towboating on the Fraser River between Hope and the Vedder Canal that **Captain Clifford Julseth** hasn't heard, the story probably isn't worth hearing. A towboating veteran with 42 years

experience, Captain Julseth has worked as deckhand, mate, skipper, dispatcher and manager. He's seen the business from all angles.

Captain Julseth lives in an attractive new house in Chilliwack, not far from the Fraser River. In 1948 he started at River Towing Company (later Rivtow Marine) on a shallow draft tug based out of Hope. He remained with the company, becoming a master in 1956 and eventually vice-president of marine operations.

On the Fraser River north of Mission, log towers need shallow draft tugs for the periods of low water. First thing in the spring, to establish whether we had enough water to tow logs down the river or not, we usually ran an exploratory trip, just two people on a boat going down carefully. Where it was extremely shallow, we'd turn around and point

Pacific Monarch alongside a flat boom. VMM

upstream, so if it became too shallow we could pull out of it. Once, just above Agassiz, we came to an area where the river channel had split into five separate channels. The most water in the one that was deep enough was in the area of three feet. A person could have actually walked across the Fraser River. That was why we needed shallow draft boats. Once the river started to rise, of course, that changed things but the boats were still quite capable of guiding their tows downriver. Towing season was mid-April to mid-October. During the winter months, at lowest water, some of the crewmen were unemployed, some found work in the lower river and Howe Sound and some worked

ashore on the river tugs' maintenance and repair. The company always kept one tug available in the water at the dock to assist the police in case of emergency.

You come out of the canyon at Hope and the river spreads but it runs over shallows and around corners as it builds gravel bars. It changes with every freshet and every winter. What was there last fall is not necessarily there in the spring. It erodes during the winter. These specially built boats were basically to get to the mouth of the Vedder Canal where it joins the Fraser River. That's where the inflowing tides meet the river's outflow and it's slack, there's no longer any tidal effect.

Four to five tugs would leave from Hope first thing in the morning, deliver down to that particular point, tie up, and return. A different style of tug, tractor tugs from down below there from Mission and New Westminster, would come and join up to maybe all four or five booms that had been delivered there the day before and take them on.

With the crews of smaller workboats working shift work, they were able to put in their time then get off the boat and go ashore to spend their off time. On the coast where the crews go aboard for, say, two weeks, their world is mostly from one end of that boat to the other. During that period they're captive. Their physical activity is somewhat limited. They are tied even while they're at work, because usually they're on duty in the wheelhouse, for instance. They're active mentally, but not much physically. There's ample food, good food. But there's even more ample coffee—caffeine users. All of this does not lead to a good healthy life. Through the years that I've spent watching the situation, there have been so many of my very good, dear friends depart. Most of them with cancer. Now whether the job bears a relationship or not, I don't know.

Tugs dock a bulk carrier at Roberts Bank. The *Seaspan Venture* is in the foreground. DM

CHAPTER 3

Wind, Waves and Weather

Towboat skippers keep a steady watch on the weather: what is happening and, more importantly, what is likely to happen. Their skill at reading sky and water for portends of change is unsurpassed; indeed, meteorologists often consult towboaters about regional weather patterns. Even with this expertise, however, towboaters get caught in foul weather. There isn't an experienced master without stories of storms that threatened tug and tow: of the ends pulled out of conky boomsticks, snapped towing straps, of scows adrift. When a storm threatens, the usual procedure for a tug and tow is to make for a sheltered bay or inlet. The speed that a tug and tow travels—two to three knots for a tug and boom—hardly warrants the word "dash" but that is exactly what it is.

The *Seaspan Venture* runs light (without a tow) in Burrard Inlet's inner harbour. DM

The difference between making it around a point to shelter, or not, is so slight that success or failure often depends on whether a deckhand fumbled a shackle, or how well the captain read the currents. Then, when the tug and tow reach shelter and are safely doing doughnuts in an inlet, urgency is replaced by boredom. The extremes of the tow-boater's life—either they are going full 'tilt or they are flat on their butts—are behind the tugboaters' saying, "Hurry up and wait."

Captain Bob McCoy *was a mate with Straits Towing when he had a memorable encounter with a storm:*

The *Magellan Straits* was a big tug of 177 tons. In November 1962, I joined her at Masset in the Queen Charlotte Islands. In those days the tugs had a seven-man crew with a cook and second engineer. We were towing a self-dumping log barge, the *Westport Straits,* between Masset and Ketchikan. This one particular day when we left, the weather forecast on Hecate Strait was good. I was off watch and asleep and when I woke the boat was acting like a Mixmaster. I got up and realized that I couldn't see anything, the air was full of spindrift, with great big seas towering in on us. When I got up to the wheelhouse the boat was laying on an angle and the tow line was over the after gunwales. The barge

Captain Larry Baese remembers being ordered to sink the hulk of the *Peerless* in 1948. When it wouldn't sink he decided to help it along by burning it: "There was a little bit of a hole through the door and it was like a huge blowtorch, with the velocity of the heat coming out. In seven minutes there was nothing left." VMM

was towing us. The captain figured the wind was blowing between 85 and 90 knots, and I was later told that they clocked it at 105 at the airport at Ketchikan that day. This damn barge had charge of us. The boat was being dragged on the starboard side by the barge. Fortunately she was a big heavy boat. The seas were so high that we could see them way above the top of the boat with spray and spindrift streaming over us. The skipper asked me to go back and check the tow line and I struggled back there and found she'd slipped almost all her tow line. There was just half a wrap of line on the winch. I got a peavey and tightened the brake up as hard as I could. I just got up to the wheelhouse a few minutes later and there was a sound like a cannon going off. The boat just leapt out of the water, came down, and she really dug herself in the first sea. The mate, Bill Church, stopped her. I went back to check and the tow line was gone. The barge was gone. Well, it was blowing so damn hard. We tried to turn, and when we did she was bursting seas over the stern so we had to turn around and head into it. We went on for two or three more hours and, just the way it does up there, the wind's gone. It moderated right down.

So we turned around and started looking for this damn barge. It was hidden in the swells. We got up to the top of one and we were nearly on top of the barge. It hadn't lost a log. Now the problem was to try and pick it up. There was a trailing line [tag line] we used to put out on the barge that was attached to a spare tow line coiled on the back. We picked up the tag line but it turned out it was made fast to the after mooring bollards on the barge instead of the tow line. The boom man at Masset had been asked to put the line over the side when he was letting the barge go. He misunderstood and had made the trailing line fast to the after bollards. Now there was no way we could tow the barge with that small line and it was dangerous in that heavy swell to try and board it. The captain, Don Lee, tried to come down on the barge so we could throw a hook line and catch it and, of course, the barge went up and the boat went down, and we broke a couple of planks on the tug. So we turned around and he backed into it. The other deckhand, Charlie Neville, had a deck line with a hook on it and he threw it. This is where the luck came in. The hook caught on the tag line between the bollards and where the big tow line was coiled up. We pulled away so hard that we broke the deck line and the heavy line snarled on the hook. So we had it. Talk about luck.

We didn't know where we were, somewhere out in Hecate Strait. The radar was shot. The only radio contact we could get was a government band. We were heading down Hecate Strait, running slow,

because this tow line wasn't that long. Finally we spotted a light flashing twice. It was Triple Island and we headed in there. When we arrived at Prince Rupert the boat was so full of water it was unbelievable. I took my mattress out and walked on it to squish the water out. The water had been coming in everywhere. I slept underneath the head that was upstairs and the water was sloshing over the edge of the toilet tank and coming down onto my bloody bunk. After we got into Prince Rupert the agent came down and he put a bottle of rum in the centre of the table and everyone just looked at it and went to bed.

Our last tow was from Port Clements to Lake Washington with a load of peeled cedar telephone poles. We delivered them all right and what happened was kind of funny, too. We were going into a lock to go up into the lake and there was a strong southerly wind blowing. They had handrails all along the side of the lock. When that log barge came up it went sideways and the logs went through the handrails. We were there all night with acetylene torches cutting these handrails off and using power saws to trim the logs. We finally got up into the lake, dumped the barge at Renton. We came out of the lake and on the way back to Vancouver, we hit another shoal and broke the tow line again. We got finished the day before Christmas. We'd been over three months with this barge. I was beginning to think Masset was my home. Of course there were days and days we couldn't get out of there. Either that or something was broken. It seemed that every time you turned around the barge man had a welding torch going. That particular barge was lost later off Kyuquot Sound when another tug had a tow line break.

The southeasterlies were the prevailing winds in the winter and were okay as long as you were going with them. I remember one time calling a captain at two or three in the morning saying, "We just got a storm warning for southeast 70." He sat up in his bed like a jack-in-the-box and yelled, "Southeast 70? My god, where are you? Where can we go?" I said, "It's not coming right away. It'll be a few hours. We're going to have to go hide." He pretty near had a heart attack.

*The storm that **Captain Alan Stanley** recalls wasn't sudden so much as it was relentless:*

A storm-bound tug may be forced to shelter in a bay for weeks at a time. SEASPAN INTERNATIONAL

We were on the *La Pointe* towing down to the Columbia River and about two days out below Cape Flattery. We weren't making any headway at all and the weather was absolutely foul with high winds. Then the wind shifted, which usually ends up worse than the previous weather. It got so bad that we had to heave-to and head into the weather. We had trouble getting up into the wind, it was so strong, and because of the strong wind the barge had the tendency to head into it. We just couldn't come around. What you have to do then is change course. The tow line is between two pins on the stern that keep it from sliding all over the place and chafing, so we had to take one of the pins out to allow more manoeuvrability before we could head around into

the wind again. Once we finally got turned into the weather, there was so much tension on the holding-down gear (it keeps the tow line between the pins and prevents it from bouncing up) that the pressure literally tore the gear loose and the tow line was bouncing up and down, up and down. I told the crew we had to get that tow line tied down somehow. So they went down below and got the block and tackles out, put the pin back in, and block and tackled the tow line down. They had just got it done and come inside the shelter deck, an enclosed area, when a rogue wave came over and took out the wheelhouse windows and the dodger [a solid railing around the outside of the wheelhouse] on that side of the tug. We had about a foot of water inside the

The *Pacific Monarch* coated in ice after a winter trip, February 1927. Freezing spray could build up until the boat was destabilized, forcing crew to attack it with picks and axes. VMM

wheelhouse. The radio and radar got washed out. The galley was right below and all the water was running down into it. For about two days out there we had no communication with anybody. The company was getting concerned because they hadn't heard from us and called the Coast Guard, who sent a plane out that circled around us then went back. We finally got into the Columbia River and delivered our tow at Portland and got our radio fixed.

The mouth of the Columbia River can be a nasty place if the weather is foul. There's so much current coming out of the river, especially on a falling tide, it gets about six or seven knots in there at times, and when the river is up really high you get more than that. It runs against the swell at the mouth of the river. We used to wait for an

The 89-foot tug *Queen* using log fenders to plough a path through sea ice, 1924. VMM

incoming tide to go up the river to cut down on the swell. During a tide change it would level right out. Sometimes there's not much swell outside but when the tide starts running against it, it really builds up.

In the winter of *1965 – 66,* ***Captain Royal Maynard*** *left the abandoned coastal mining town of Anyox, BC towing a barge of derelict mining equipment:*

It was blowing fairly hard, about 40 knots, but it just kept increasing as we went down Portland Inlet. It got so strong that two fellows, each weighing about 200 pounds, couldn't open the back door of the wheelhouse against the force of the wind. We finally got into Khutzeymateen Inlet and spent two days in there waiting for the wind to decrease. The boat that I was running at the time would only make nine knots with-

Capt. Royal Maynard, February 2003. JUNE MAYNARD PHOTO

out a tow and make seven to seven and a half knots with a tow. We were at a little less than half speed with the sea that was running so we wouldn't break the tow line, and we were making 11½ knots coming down there with the wind behind us. This gives some indication of the strength of the wind.

Many years later, in November sometime in the 1990s, I was skipper on the *Escort Protector*, a tug of about 170 feet with 3,200 horsepower, and we were heading for Haines, Alaska, towing an empty log barge, the *Rivtow Carrier*, 369 feet long and 76 feet wide. The night before had been about 50 degrees Fahrenheit and raining. I got to bed at midnight and we were running fairly easy because we had a time set up for arriving there at 10 o'clock in the morning. About 1:30 a.m. the wind was howling and ice was crashing on the deck and we were pulling full and just about going nowhere. The wind was up to about 70 knots outflow and very cold. When we arrived in Haines that morning,

November 21st, right at the dock it was blowing 40 knots. It made for a difficult landing. We were iced down, about a foot of ice all over the boat, including the pipe handrailings. Even the shrouds going up to the mast were 10 times their size. We didn't get any logs loaded that day because it was so cold they couldn't get the cranes running on the barge. We finally got them operating that night and started loading the next morning. It took a day and a half to get the load on because of the conditions. It usually takes about 10 hours. So we left there on the afternoon of the 22nd of November. The morning of the 24th we were bucking southeast storm-force winds down Clarence Strait. Of course it didn't get light until about nine o'clock in the morning up there. The barge was hanging off to the portside and as it started getting light I saw that it had about a 15-foot list to port. We pulled into Sunny Bay, which is part of Ernest Sound, about 40 miles north of Ketchikan, to try and ascertain why the barge had this list. I dropped the mate, the second engineer and one deckhand on the barge and they couldn't find any water in the hull so it meant that one of the tipping tanks had

Modern electronic aids like radar and GPS have made the tugboat skipper's life a lot easier, but towing in fog still quickens the pulse, especially in close quarters.
WWW.PACIFICWEBSITES. COM

water in it. That's how they dump the barge, by filling the tanks and tipping it. By this time we had people in Vancouver alerted and we had several people arriving up there. The trouble was we couldn't dump the barge to find out what was wrong with it until we had boomsticks to corral the logs that would be coming off. It was another two days before we had enough boomsticks to do this. A tug from Wrangell, Alaska went and got them. We finally dumped the barge and there was a stress crack in the deck, which had gone right around its curve and about 10 feet down the side of the hull and had let water into one of the tipping tanks. We suspected that the crack had been started by the extreme cold and bad weather we experienced getting up there. The stress of loading and the travelling after that had made it spread. It cost about two and a half days of no sleep at all, for me anyway, because every time I closed my eyes I could see the whole thing dumping and no sticks in the area. We were carrying a few million bucks worth of wood, 10,000 tons, and if it dumped with no sticks to contain it, it would be very hard to retrieve.

Rivers, especially small ones like the Courtenay, present tug skippers with some of the trickiest navigation challenges. Here a local tug pulls a tow of logs past the range marker.
WWW.PACIFICWEBSITES.COM

After getting the load off the barge, corralling the wood with boomsticks, tying it all to the shore and leaving a small American tug to keep watch, we took the empty barge down and met another tug with a different barge, at Namu, and traded barges. He took the crippled barge back to Vancouver and we took the other one back to Sunny Bay and reloaded. Eventually we got it to its destination, Gold River on Vancouver Island.

Another time, at the top end of the Charlottes, we were running slow, waiting tide to get into Naden Harbour and a northeasterly was coming up out of Portland Canal. It was 60 to 70 knots. We were running with a fairly short line, maybe 900 feet of tow line out. I was standing at the back of the wheelhouse, watching the lines to make sure they weren't straining too much, and our bow came up on a swell and pushed our stern down approximately eight feet under water. Then the bow came down off that wave. This great mass of water on the 90-foot-long stern deck ran forward toward the houseworks, then the next swell came right over the bow. So here we were getting it from both ends. Our next move was to run some tow line out and head for the west coast of the Charlottes for shelter. That was the first time I'd ever run to the west coast for shelter.

On a different trip we were out on the west coast loading at Zeballos and got about half a load there, then moved over to Nesook Bay in Nootka Sound area and took the other half-load, then anchored for weather because it was blowing very hard outside, 70 to 80 knots. There was no wind at all where we anchored and the mate was at the stern of the barge securing its anchor. In the two and a half to three minutes it took the mate to come forward from the stern of the barge I heard this cracking noise. I couldn't tell where it was coming from. I thought it might be the engineer doing something down below. It turned out to be trees breaking off and uprooting from a tremendous gust of wind, about a half-mile away. A whole swath of trees went down. When that wind hit the water it was just unbelievable the disturbance it caused. Of course the next move was to get the engines going again and send the mate back to the stern of the barge, raise the anchor and get out into a less confined area. When the wind actually hit us, there was so much water in the air you couldn't see five feet. It wasn't rain, it was water that the wind had picked up from the ocean. We spent the next three days running slow inside Nootka Sound until the weather abated.

*As **Captain Alan Wood** recalls, storms were only one challenge the tow-boater faced:*

Years ago, coming up and down the coast before the tugs had radar, in thick fog we'd use the ship's whistle. We'd count the number of seconds it would take for the whistle to echo off the shore. We could go anywhere just using the echo. When I worked in the harbour, deep-sea ships used to come in and they didn't have radar either. On the tug, we could find the ship in the fog by using the whistle and the echo would bounce off the hull. The ship also found the dock he was going to by having one of the tugs go over to that particular dock and stand off either end, whichever end the pilot requested, and we'd continue to blow the whistle, blow once, and wait two or three seconds and blow it again, and the ship would come right into the dock, heading for the sound.

Coming out of English Bay in the fog, coming into First Narrows and still using the whistle, as long as we kept the echo off of Prospect Point to one second, we could come into the harbour and as we came

Powerful Tiger Tugz docking tug tends a bulk carrier at the Cascadia grain terminal. The strong tidal currents at Second Narrows in Burrard Inlet can make ship handling tricky.
MARV PELKEY PHOTO

around Prospect Point and into Brockton Point, the land slopes in a
little so the echo would increase to two seconds. As we got nearer to
Brockton Point, the land comes out again and the echo would drop to
one second again. Then we would head for the dock. Some of the
docks had whistles and some had bells at the end. So we just headed
to the sound.

On October 16, 1979, I had a traumatic experience in the fog,
even with radar. The vessel *Japan Erica* was taking on a load of raw logs
at Goodwin Johnson, which was just at the other side of Second
Narrows Bridge. We were sent up from the foot of Lonsdale on the
Cates VII to tend the ship. When we left our dock it was thick fog as
we headed to Goodwin Johnson. When it came time to pull the ship
from the dock, the pilot ordered us to put a tow line on its stern, and
in the process of the ship letting its lines go, they dropped all three
stern lines and at that precise moment the ship tried its engines out,

On the night of October 16,
1979, in a thick fog, the ship
Japan Erica hit the Second
Narrows railway bridge in Burrard
Inlet. Captain Alan Wood was on
a tug tending the ship.
PHOTO ELLSWORTH DICKSON, NORTH
SHORE NEWS

which meant the propeller was turning and two lines got caught in the ship's propeller. She was 20 or 30 feet off the dock, and we were told to try and pull the ship's line out of the wheel, which we couldn't do. They decided to go ahead anyway with the line in the wheel because the power was strong enough that it didn't really bother them that much and it would probably burn off.

All this time it was still thick fog. The pilot ordered us to stand by to Second Narrows, which we did. We started down toward the narrows and I was stationed about six feet back from the bow of the ship. There was absolutely no visibility and it was between nine and 10 o'clock at night. The first thing I saw was the pillar on the bridge, which I thought was the south end, which it should have been if we were right on course. I told the pilot and in about two or three seconds the ship hit the railway bridge. There was a tremendous crash and electric wires flashing. The whole area turned blue with flashes. I backed

The 160-horsepower tug *Our Best* uses log fenders to break a path through sea ice off Port Moody after Burrard Inlet froze in 1942. CAPTAIN CECIL J. RHODES PHOTO

about 20 or 25 feet away from the ship, lost contact with it and took a few minutes to find it again. We went over off Cates Park with it, where it anchored. I took the pilot back to Vancouver. At work the next morning we were shocked to see that the north tower of the railway bridge was leaning about 30 feet out of alignment.

It took about a year to get it repaired and it cut off the North Shore from the usual railway traffic over the bridge. Some businesses were close to going bankrupt because their goods—the sulphur, coal, grain and other supplies that were brought over on the rail bridge from the south shore—had to be brought on train barges to keep the North Shore going until trains could be rerouted south through Squamish.

The winters used to bring some special problems. When we were pulling tows up to Woodfibre or Squamish and the outflow winds were blowing at their best down Howe Sound, the whole tug would be coated in thick ice that formed from the waves blowing up over the side. The crews had a dangerous time when they had to go out on the deck and tie up. In Burrard Inlet, when we were called out during or after a snowstorm, the decks would be thick with snow, making footing treacherous. We would pull up to a freighter that was discharging hot water from a six-inch hole in the hull and get under the stream of water, letting it run down the starboard deck, then the port deck, then turn the tug around and let the water melt the snow off of the stern. It worked really well. Everybody did it. A lot of ice used to form on Seymour Inlet during the winter. In order to break through to get at our tows, we used a special device to protect our bows from damage. We would attach two boomsticks in a V down each side of the

bow, connected at the point with a boom chain and on each side of the tug with wire straps. It worked well and certainly saved our wooden hulls from gouges.

For as long as tugs have worked the coast, Skookumchuck Narrows has held a special place in towboating lore. The tide rushes through the narrow passage in Sechelt Inlet and creates boiling rapids and whirlpools four times a day. **Captain Howie Keast** knows the area well:

Skookumchuck Narrows is no place to fool around in heavy tides. I have been through the narrows both ways with heavily loaded gravel barges going north and empty barges heading south into the narrows. Even after working out the times of slack water you could still be a little bit wrong due to the weather outside. Fortunately for me I never got into any trouble. However, others did. I was called up by Rivtow

When Capt. Westmoreland received his master's ticket in 1957 the *Jean L.* was the first tug he captained. Here she tows past Point Atkinson Lighthouse at the entrance to Burrard Inlet; a trustworthy beacon since 1912, the lighthouse is now automated. VMM

Straits to figure out some safe way to navigate through the narrows. This was in desperation due to the insuring involved in the accidents in the past. First they suggested buoys, and I vetoed that because sometimes the back eddies moved the buoys and they would give wrong readings. I suggested a small water taxi from Egmont to sit in the narrows shortly before slack water and let us know when the tide was slackened up, which they did, and we went through. To my knowledge there has never been another accident with gravel barges passing through the narrows.

Skookumchuck Narrows is very dangerous when the tide is running; there are swirls and undercurrents and even at slack water the current is still running under the surface. You have to be very careful. This is why we were so cautious running through there with the heavy barges. If you got into trouble, you were in real trouble and usually the barge sank. Weather was a big factor. If there was southeast weather

Seaspan Tempest takes green water coming home from Roberts Bank in a westerly, ca. 1980s. K. STEIMAN PHOTO

outside in Georgia Strait there was a difference in the tide, and when you figured the tide out at slack water and the weather was not taken into consideration, then you could be way out. In the summertime, when the tides are big, like 13-foot floods, Rapid Island in the middle with a light trembles and you can hear the tide running in the narrows a half-mile away.

When I was on the *Jean L.* we used to tow logs from Vancouver Island to Vancouver, Howe Sound and what have you. We took a tow from Howe Sound over to Nanaimo. The weather was terrific when we left and we had a good trip for halfway across. When the weather report came on it forecast for gales of southeast. In a short time, we were only about five miles from Entrance Island, the wind came up with big swells. Of course my booms were starting to deplete. I knew we were picking up speed because we were losing the logs. I got a call on the radio from our office asking if I knew the gale warning had been posted. I said, "Oh, it has, has it? Just for your information, we're already in it." However, when we got into Nanaimo we only had the boomsticks left and the logs were scattered all around the Winchelsea Islands. So I got hold of the L & K log department and asked them to close the area to shipping. We got the beachcombers out. There was one fellow we relied on quite a bit and he would look after it. In two days he had all of the logs picked up because they were all in puddles and groups all around the Winchelseas. The logging department boss told me it was the best thing that ever happened. Between the insurance and the loss of the logs and the other arrangements that were made we were far ahead of the value of the logs when we first started out because of the transactions that took place. So they made more money on the job than they would have if we had completed the tow.

Aboard a Norwegian deep-sea vessel, **Captain Aage Fransvaag** *had seen plenty of foul weather. But a storm experienced in a freighter and a storm experienced in a tug with a tow are dramatically different:*

In the days when they were building the first oil rig in Esquimalt in the mid-sixties, we were dispatched down to San Francisco Bay to pick up a big heavy-lift crane on a 2,000-ton capacity barge and tow it up to Victoria. At that time the whole coast was involved in exploration for Shell. The *Sedco 135F* was the name of the oil rig. The company had their own exploration boats and supply ships, the *Min Tide* and the *Canadian Tide*, built in Canada. The drilling started off at Tofino in 14 fathoms and went all the way up to Triple Island in Hecate Strait. The

The *Gulf Joan* of Gulf of Georgia
Towing, with the Shell Oil drilling
rig *Sedco 135F*, up the west
coast, 1967.

Gulf of Georgia vessel *Gulf Joan* was the primary tug, the *Sudbury II*
was there occasionally, the *Harold A. Jones*, and Straits company had
most of their tugs involved. It was not often you had three tugs pulling
this rig. They had their own specialties. The weather in that period,
about nine months, was the worst weather I think I've ever seen on any
ocean. It was even worse than the North Sea on the Norwegian navy

ships where there was the same depth, 25 fathoms, as in Hecate Strait. It builds up some short tremendous swells. It was the same, week after week, the same horrible weather.

Another time I was with Captain Don Chatt off Cape St. James at Hecate Strait. I have never seen worse weather. The rig master told us when he dismissed us that there was a 55-foot swell underneath the oil rig and we were contemplating abandoning it. We wanted to just stand off for a while. One of the tugs actually lost a lifeboat. The wind gusted to over 125 knots and blew off the American wind gauge on top of our mast. She was screaming. It was probably something that a born West-Coaster could be used to, but to me it was very unusual. We were dismissed and the captain took us into Jedway. It's an abandoned

Tug tows a salt barge from Long Beach, California through broken ice on the Fraser River, 1989.
TED KING COLLECTION

mine/ore facility close to Cape St. James. Don managed to get into this partially floating cement dock. It was blowing so hard we had to crawl, holding on to each other to get the wires from the boat onto the dock. Everything was just white with the spray and the wind. A couple of hours later the two supply ships, the *Min Tide* and the *Canadian Tide*, came in. I was up in the wheelhouse with the captain and they were talking by radio: "Could we come in and tie up to you?" The captain said: "I don't think that would be a good idea." That particular winter—about 1965—weatherwise was absolutely horrible.

Captain Donald MacPherson *recalls that spring freshets on the Fraser River caused unique problems:*

Just to illustrate the strength of the freshet, it would take us eight hours and 20 minutes to run the vessels light from New Westminster to Mission. However, we would come down with three loads in just three hours and 20 minutes. All we were doing was steering the tow. We had to be very careful to keep to the deepest part of the river. They call it reading the water. But you can tell by the way the river runs where the deep water is and figure the best way to travel. You can generally tell by the banks of the river on the bends where the silt is carried away and the water is deeper because the river is running faster up against the bank and has more strength. In 1948, when the freshet raised the level at Mission to 24.7 feet, the river scoured a new channel below Mission 40 to 60 feet deep that had never been there before. A great deal of caution had to be observed when tying up a tow in the river, especially in high water conditions. We were on 12-hour shifts—six to six or seven to seven—around the clock and when a new crew came on they usually drove to the Shell dock at New Westminster, which was our normal crew-change station. But especially at freshet time, we had to let them know where the tug was because you couldn't always predict how long the trip would take. They'd take a taxi to meet up with the tug at its location.

The worst weather on the river was fog but crosswinds were hard to deal with when you were running a bridge. They would catch the tow like a sail. Weather never held us up on the river, though. We would go out no matter what the weather and do the best we could. But on Burrard Inlet, before we had radar and we were in fog going through Second Narrows, we made radio contact with the bridge operator who would count out loud continuously through a loudhailer so that we could steer toward the sound of his voice. At First Narrows

"On October 22, 1968, *SEDCO 135F*, an oil-drilling rig anchored west of Cape St. James at the southern tip of the Queen Charlotte Islands, was battered by 20-metre (65-foot) waves. As a monster wave approached, a lower support form of the rig was exposed. The following wave crest passed just below a control room located 30.4 metres (100 feet) above the support form. More recently, Pacific storms have produced gigantic waves—perhaps the largest ever measured by instruments—just offshore…. The danger of these waves is not simply due to the incredible height of the crest above the trough. Their sudden growth results in very steep sides. Survivors have described the steep trough ahead of, or behind, a freak wave as a 'hole in the sea.' The wave itself is often described as an overhanging 'wall' of water that seemed to stretch from horizon to horizon."

David Jones, meteorologist, Environment Canada, quoted in *The Westcoast Mariner*, November 1996

there was a little shack in the middle of Lions Gate Bridge for the traffic controllers. We kept in touch with them by radio and they would inform us of known traffic.

Fraser River pilot **Captain Ted King**:

Steam tug *Annie* grounded at the foot of Denman St., in English Bay, Vancouver around the beginning of the last century..
CVA

We have problems with every kind of weather constantly on the Fraser River. Sometimes you have zero visibility with snow. You and nature— who is going to win? Wind is really a bad thing. With any kind of a ship or barges, wind is one of your main enemies. Sometimes we used

to work for two weeks solid in the fog on the river. I remember going to work and depending for two weeks on radar. Your eyeballs were ready to fall out of your head at the end of that time—dropping barges and picking them up and trying to run the bridges.

One year the river froze so bad that we'd tow a barge full speed into a dock and never stop the engine. We'd put the tug into neutral and the ice stopped the tug and the barge. I remember walking on the ice in New Westminster and having to tie a barge up by using a fire axe to cut a boom chain out that was frozen and shackle it into the chain. In those days we had a lot of ice. One time in the 80s we had a real severe winter, and I remember going up to McMillan Slough [now McDonald Slough] with an empty barge. It was a beautiful, beautiful, crystal clear night, ice everywhere. We were just coming around the corner. There are big homes up there on the bluff. There was solid ice across the slough. So we put quite a bit of line out to slow the barge down for a minute and crashed into that ice. I tell you, with a steel tug the noise was horrendous. Every porch light for miles around lit up. You could see people on the decks of all the houses looking down. Then we'd back the tug up and make another run at it. And back the tug up. You could hear all this ice crashing and cracking. We broke the mouth of the slough open and we went through with the barge up to the mill. We sure hoped that the ice was still clear when we went back down with a full barge so we could keep on going.

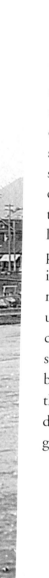

Every year between mid-May and early July, snowmelt and rain in BC's interior cause water levels on the lower Fraser River to peak. Nearly 30 times in the last 125 years, freshets have raised the river in the Hope to Mission run more than 20 feet above its usual level; in 1948 the river was measured at 24.7 feet above normal. For towboaters, high water and high velocity mean there is more debris in the river, increasing the risk of snarled propellers and steering nozzles, or strained tie-up lines and structures. It is the most dangerous season to work on the river.

Pleasure Craft, Bridges and Other Headaches

Compared with the often strange manoeuvres of sports boats and yachts, West Coast weather seems pleasantly predictable. Most tugboat masters would rather face a regular gale than a bay full of recreational boats run by inexperienced, sometimes drunken operators. Too often there seems to be no reason to what anglers or sailors do: they turn in front of a tug, ignoring the fact that it cannot suddenly alter course or stop; they'll get between a bluff and a boom (a certain way to pulverize a fibreglass hull); or, famously, they'll cross between tug and tow, unaware that they risk losing their prop—or worse—to the tow line. There are bridges, on-board fires, or errant barges—all disasters in waiting for the towboater.

The tug *Lorne*'s barge, the *Pacific Gatherer*, caught in an eddy, dislodges the Second Narrows bridge in Burrard Inlet, September 19, 1930. "It was the biggest damn splash anybody has ever seen," said the *Lorne*'s captain, Barney Johnson, who watched in horror as the 8,000-ton span of the bridge tumbled into the narrows. CVA

Captain Royal Maynard:

A small charter boat came alongside us just before midnight and wanted to know where Pender Harbour was. I had him tie up alongside and he came on board and I showed him on the chart where Pender Harbour was and where he was. He had his wife and three- or four-year-old son in the boat. He said, "Oh, I can't understand those maps. Just a minute." He went into his boat and came back with a road map. This is what he was navigating by. I was a little disgusted. I told him he should head for the lights south of us, which was Vancouver, and go home before he ended up killing his wife and family.

Many years ago we were going into West Bay, Howe Sound with a tow of logs about three o'clock in the morning and there was a 60- to 70-foot yacht tied up in an open section between three booms in the storage grounds out there where we would be trying to tie this tow up. I blew the whistle and woke the fellow up. I talked to him and told him he had to move and he was extremely rude and used several words that we won't print. He refused to move. I said, fine, don't move then. We tied the tow up and he had no way out. It was on a Friday night in early fall and I guess he finally got out some time Monday when the boom men from the sorting grounds showed up.

We used to see some strange things in the summertime working in Howe Sound. People didn't use much common sense. They'd come out on weekends and have parties and actually start campfires on the log booms. But they didn't always put them out. Many times we had to put fires out on the booms after a weekend.

We saw many problems with fish boats, too. On one trip north to Kitimat just a couple of years ago, we overtook and passed a 40- to 45-foot fish boat in Lama Pass.

I went to bed just after we passed him. When I got up in the morning the mate said, "Oh, that boat that we passed last night sank. It must have hit German Point." We got up nearer Kitimat and there was another fish boat washed up on the beach. We loaded the barge in Kitimat and headed back toward Howe Sound, and in Tolmie Channel there was a good-sized fish boat, 80 feet or better, that had hit Hewitt Island and was upside down drifting around out there. It eventually sank in deep water. Then we got down to Johnstone Strait and there's another big fish boat with his bow right up in the trees. He must have gone to sleep and hit the shore at high water. When we passed him there was no water touching the boat at all.

Captain Joe Quilty *was probably the only West Coast towboat skipper who was regularly the target of friendly fire*:

During the Second World War, I was in the army, and because I had my master's ticket, they made me skipper on the *General Lake*, the target-towing tug on the West Coast. The tow line was a mile long and made of three-eighths-inch wire, with a high-speed winch that reeled in the line at 16 knots while the tug steamed at 16 knots, giving the

Army tug *General Lake* worked towing targets during WWII, surviving some errant shots itself. VMM

target a speed of 32 knots for a short time. The target was a sort of sled, designed to throw a rooster comb about six feet above the target, which was what the gunners aimed at. The idea was not to hit the target but to bracket it. We would start out at Victoria, tow there for the shore batteries, then go to Vancouver where they had six-inch guns on Point Grey and then to First Narrows where they had 12-pounders covering the entrance to the harbour. We always did a night tow for them. Then we'd go from there to Yorke Island, about halfway up the east coast of Vancouver Island, where they had a coastal defence battery of six-inch guns. From there we'd go to Prince Rupert, then back down and do the whole thing over again. The tug never got hit but some shots did come pretty close.

*Captain **Adrian Bull** has many stories about West Coast towboating, all flavoured with the distinctive sounds of his Scottish accent. It is especially delightful if those stories happen to include a vessel or vessels with an R in the name; no one matches his pronunciation, for example, of the barge* Forest Prince. *Captain Bull joined Island Tug & Barge in 1962 after 12 years on deep-sea vessels. He was skipper for eight years, then came ashore. He remains active as a volunteer with the Maritime Museum of British Columbia in Victoria.*

Capt. Adrian Bull, 1967.

If you really want knuckle-biters go into the Columbia River at [US] Thanksgiving, November on a foggy day. As you come down and make your turn around No. 1 buoy, you shorten up, and you look in the radar and all you can see are blips—all you can see! The bigger blips are the buoys, the smaller ones are yachts. You can see where you want to go and you just keep going because you can't stop. As you go by the buoy where these guys are—they want to go home now, eh?—foggy weather—you can see them peeling off coming toward you following the sound of the whistle and you end up with a whole string of yachts behind you—thousands it seems like. As you work your way in, there's an idiot who's caught a fish, and there's no way he's gonna move. So you come alongside and you nudge him out of the way with the tug because you can't do anything else. And you watch it. There's three guys on the boat usually—one is pushing off the hull, another guy is clubbing the fish to death. You are really scared because you've got a great big 12x12 sticking out the side of your boat—the rubbing strake. He's going to catch that at some point when you roll. You just bite your nails hoping that he'll be kicked out from under so you won't sink him. Then as you get farther in, the fog lifts a little bit and the yachts break away and disappear to points around there. There's always an idiot who's broken down. You can see him. He's right ahead of you and he's standing there, not moving, not doing anything. You call the Coast Guard and say, "Hey, there's a guy out here and he's broken down." You have to keep going, you can't stop. So you ease around him with the tug, then you look back aft and you watch the barge coming right at him. And it hits him. He's under the chain but you have to keep going because if you stop the chain drops and he's caught. It scares the hell out of you. It really does. That's the way it is on the Columbia River bar at Thanksgiving. Every year it's the same thing. Sometimes I thought it wasn't worth it the way you'd sweat. You watch these guys and there's nothing you can do. You just have to keep going. They won't move, they just fish. They don't give a damn for anything. It's really amazing. My wife could always tell if I'd had a good trip or a bad trip by the number of jerks I'd give in my sleep.

The anonymous retired skipper:

Maybe I'm a little heavy on it, but I've been fighting those buggers for 35 years—fishermen and yachtsmen. But the one I almost got, we were in Vancouver doing a bollard pull. I was on the *Seaspan Monarch* at Centerm, the container port. It was a test to see how hard the tug pulled. We'd put the tow line up on bollards on the dock, move ahead, run a couple hundred feet of tow line and just do a steady pull. The engineers used a dynamometer to see how hard the boat pulled. And of all people it was the Vancouver bloody police boat started to cross the tow line. I blew the whistle. Nothing happened. I eventually stopped the boat, which of course blew their test all to hell because it takes some time to set this thing up. I had to drop the tow line. The police boat never knew. I was so close to the dock they shouldn't have come between anyway. Maybe that's why they haven't got one any more. Whatta you do?

I had a skipper once that used to say, "The quickest way to kill a yachtsman is to teach him the rules of the road." They start insisting on their rights and it's got nothing to do with rights. People in small

The *Seaspan Monarch*, previously the *Harold A. Jones* of Vancouver Tugboat Co., awaits launching at Vancouver Shipyards in North Vancouver. DM

Opposite: The dented bow of *La Pointe* after an accident, October 21, 1942. VMM

boats don't realize that if the barge touches somebody, they're gonna die. It's nothing to do with who has the right of way. They're not going to get their feet wet, they're probably going to die. When you get in front of a barge, you don't bounce off. You usually go right underneath it and pop out the back. The US Coast Guard, down Puget Sound, have traffic lanes and the rule down there is that the pleasure craft will stay the hell out of the way of the commercial traffic. It's the only rule. Stay out of the bloody way. The US Coast Guard enforces it. They don't mess around.

The "buggers" that the anonymous captain mentions sometimes include commercial fishermen. **Captain Aage Fransvaag:**

I was bound for Nootka Sound with three loaded chip barges on the *Seaspan Navigator*. Heavy fog. I just came around Race Rocks to line up with the traffic lanes. You could see two fish boats on the radar screen. All of a sudden one of them came across my bow and dropped

his net. Five thousand dollars. No court case, just pay up. No sense in arguing. Lucky I didn't take out the fish boat. We feel he did it on purpose so they could put in a claim. If the fishing is not good enough they apparently dump an old net overboard and the tug runs over it—five thousand dollars. One skipper came down the river with chip barges and took out seven nets. You can't stop, you just have to keep on going.

Capt. Hugh Wallace, ca. 1980.
MARTIN BEDFORD PHOTO

*The maritime tradition that Charles Henry Cates founded in BC endures in the career of his grandson, **Captain Hugh Wallace**. A quietly professional man, Captain Wallace has worked for the firm his grandfather founded—C.H. Cates & Sons Limited—most of his career in Vancouver harbour. Captain Wallace started working part time at C.H. Cates & Sons in 1959 at the age of 15. Later he worked full time as a deckhand and in the company shop. He received his master's ticket in 1972 and has since worked on many of the company's harbour tugs. Captain Wallace lives in North Vancouver.*

One time when I was docking, the CN dock was on fire. We went over to tow away boats and scows tied up there. The heavy black creosote smoke was so thick I could hardly breathe. One morning in October 1975, I was walking up Cates' dock and heard a loud boom. I looked to the east and saw a cloud of smoke so I ran into our dispatch office. They said that Burrard Terminal had just had an explosion. So we ran down and jumped on a boat and headed over there. A ship was tied to the dock and the workhouse of the elevator was burning. We got the ship to take our tow lines and to throw their tie-up lines off. We were at the stern and another tug was at the bow. The ship's crew wouldn't let the last tie-up line go. Someone went up on the dock and chopped the line and we towed the ship out off the dock and stood by. Later a pilot came out and got aboard the ship. The fire got bigger and bigger and four or five firemen got trapped on the dock, but the Harbour Patrol boat went and got them off. The fire continued growing; I had never seen such a huge fire. There were sheets of corrugated iron flying up from the draft and floating down all over. I saw a fellow running across the railroad tracks and this big sheet was floating down. I thought it was going to land on him. When just the wooden frame of the workhouse was left it all collapsed in a huge orange fireball. The old Vancouver fireboat arrived with its whistles blowing. The water pressure was so powerful from the fireboat that it could blow the siding off of the buildings. Nothing else was as effective as the fireboat.

The fire was out a short time later. Six men died and several were severely burned.

Our company did a lot of work around Burrard Dry Dock when the ferries were being built there. They extended some of them by cutting them in half, building new sections and floating the new sections in. I remember walking up our dock early one quiet Sunday morning

The *Seaspan Stormer* runs a ship's line to tie-up at Roberts Bank. Skippers have to be alert to avoid being crushed by massive ships. ca. 1980s. DM

[in October 1980] and I heard a big crunching sound over by the dry dock. I ran into the office and told them the ferry had just fallen over on the dry dock and we were going over. When we got there the ferry [*Queen of Coquitlam*] was lying against the side of the dry dock and had a hole in its hull. We could see that the dry dock was slowly sinking. If the weight of the ferry had broken the side of the dock it seemed that the boat could roll off against a new ferry that was being built beside it. A few men were working inside the ferry at the time and somebody said they were calling for help on a different radio channel. Since it was Sunday it took a while for the other shipyard workers to get there. When they arrived they told us to hook onto the new ferry that was being built and tow it out and not worry about the gangway, welding cables and ladders, etc. So we put on our tow line and started pulling. There were wires snapping and ladders falling. We towed it clear of the dock and stood by it. The ferry's rudder got snagged on one of the marker buoys that were put in for the new dry dock that was coming from Japan. It took some time for the diver to free the cable. Meanwhile they sank the dry dock to right the ferry and float it off but it had a hole in its hull from falling over. I believe they sealed off that

Seaspan tugs docking a large bulk-carrier at Roberts Bank in the late 1980s. DM

compartment. Evidently part of the engine room was flooded causing water damage to some of the electrical machinery.

The tie-up lines aboard the deep-sea ships are very heavy. One of the tugs would usually pick up the lines from the bow and stern of the ship and run them into the longshoremen while the other tugs held the ship alongside the dock. There were usually four lines on each end of the ship. One day I was decking on the line boat with a new skipper. We were told to ask the pilot when we could pick up the lines. About a year before, a ship's anchor had dropped on the stern of one of the tugs that sank but everyone got off. I told the new skipper to ask the pilot's permission to pick up the lines before we went under the anchor so that he would know that we were there. We backed under the anchor and I grabbed two lines. I heard a click and some of the clay from the anchor landed on the back deck. I walked backwards with the lines and the anchor started coming down. I tripped over the wheel-house doorsill and fell on my back inside. The anchor turned and just missed the tug. A big splash of water came up and soaked me while I was lying on my back. The linesman started laughing at me.

Captain Donald MacPherson, *the sometime magician, photographer and long-time towboater:*

Everybody working on the Fraser River had unforgettable experiences, close shaves. I was really fortunate that I didn't have too many. It takes a good deal of diligence to operate tugs safely. I had some trouble with fish boats in the main river above New Westminster. They put out their nets and they want you to go around them, but it's impossible. Often they don't carry proper lights. If they don't have the white light on the end of their net you can't tell where the net is. In the river their shallow-draft boats were drifting fairly rapidly with their nets. There's no way you can go around them because you don't have enough water. I often went through nets but nobody liked to do that.

One time we were coming down through the Fraser Avenue bridge with a chip barge. There were about 600 yards between the Fraser Avenue and Twigg Island swingspans. A large deadhead jammed the tug's stern causing the barge to drive the tug around to the barge's starboard corner. To remedy the situation, we ran a tow line to the other end of the barge and snapped on the winch brake. I gave the engine full throttle, turning the barge so that it was now facing upriver. There was barely enough room to turn it. You could easily have stepped off the barge onto the protection pier of the Twigg Island railway bridge.

Three tugs docking a salt barge from Mexico, ca. 1980s. DM

Captain Ted King:

I had fished, so the fish boats don't bother me. I can almost contemplate what a fisherman's going to do. I only ever remember hitting one net. It used to be quite funny because a lot of the skippers were quite nervous of the fish boats, so they used to ask me to steer because I knew the area around Steveston so well. So I'd be going down the river with the window open and I'd yell, "Hey Joe, get your net out of the way."

The North Arm of the Fraser River used to be absolutely solid logs and barges. One time on the *Le Prince* we had two barges behind us, and we came up through the BC Hydro bridge in Marpole, next to Oak Street Bridge. There were log tows everywhere. Just solid log towers. So we had to stop the barges up because we had no place to go. We stopped. We were at Mitchell Island at Mitchell Slough. The tide was flooding. So the log tows started pushing our barges. We were sitting with our nose on the beach at Twigg tie-up with the tow line attached to the barges and they were being pushed up Mitchell Slough on the other side of the island. On the tug we were running her tow line and just sat there drinking coffee. It all finally came to a stop when the log towers pulled back on their tows. So we started heaving our tow line in and carried on with our trip.

We don't usually go up the river past Mission. There's a very anti-
quated railway bridge there. It has a very narrow opening and the tide
runs up there like you wouldn't believe. That's one bridge where you
used to tell your mate, "I don't want you to talk to me, or do anything.
Just stand there, and when I tell you to do something, do it." It was
called the "White Knuckle Trip."

One time in the late '60s, when I was working on the river, a barge
was being towed down and knocked the old Fraser Avenue bridge out.
It took the whole centre span out. Cars were in the water. Someone
had misjudged the height. They put a Bailey bridge across and all river
traffic had to get diverted up and down Mitchell Slough. It was quite
exciting. You had to be very accurate in estimating the height of the

The Marpole bridge across the
Fraser River to Lulu Island opens
to allow BridgeTowing's tug
Pullaway to pass through with a
tow, May 16, 1952. PHOTO CROTON
STUDIO, VPL

Bridges add to the challenge of towing on the Fraser River. The shallow draft tug *Red Fir 9* of River Towing in foreground. CMC

bridges and you had to know how high your barges were. When you were heading up the North Arm, you had to count the number of planks at Oak Street Bridge showing above the water and you added 19 feet to that, which gave you the clearance at the Fraser Avenue bridge. So you had to make up your mind real quickly when you went through the bridge whether you'd go that way or go through Mitchell Slough, where there were no overhead obstructions. So you'd figure out the height of all your barges, decide which was the highest one, say, 26 feet, so you'd know how many planks you'd need to give enough clearance for 26 feet. I remember one night my skipper and I came down from the Fraser Mills with a covered barge. The skipper always liked to run very close to the line, so I told him that this barge wasn't going to clear the bridge because I'd put kerosene lamps on the top of it at each

corner, so the barge was a little higher than it was supposed to be. He was sure everything would be okay but I bet him a buck that we wouldn't clear the bridge. So we come under the bridge and it knocked all of the kerosene lamps off. I said, "You owe me a buck."

Captain Larry Baese:

One Christmas season when I was working on the *Coyle No. 3*, we were coming home and Doug Coyle, the owner and dispatcher, called us and wanted us to go up to New Westminster to pick up this tug. We got up there and, of course, the tug's motor had been shut down for some time and they'd left the rudder hard over when they'd tied the boat up originally. So we got ahold of it and started down the river

A Vantug tug tows a Northland barge on a short line near the mouth of the Fraser River's North Arm, late 1950s. A short tow line gives better control of the barge, but also increases chances of the barge overtaking the tug. DM

The powerful *Pacific Monarch* could handle heavy tows in high seas, but was just as vulnerable as any boat when she touched bottom on a falling tide. VMM

towing it alongside our tug but we couldn't steer either one even though ours was diesel. Because the tug was steam steering and there was no steam on, you couldn't put the rudder amidships. Then we had all those bridges to deal with. We had a bridge at Queensborough, the train bridge, and two bridges at Marpole to go through. Finally we had to have the engineers get two big steel bars and go into the engine room and bar the steam steering over until they got the rudder amidships so we could control the tow. It was a pretty wild, snowy, windy night and we shot through the bridges. That was a real feat, having two

tugs tied alongside each other like this to go through those narrow spans. I remember at the BC Hydro bridge the skipper came into it really slow and he put the *Coyle No. 3* against the sheer that protects the bridge's supports and just crept through it because there wasn't enough room. But we got it down and we got out of the river. We had pretty bad weather, so we couldn't keep the tugs alongside each other, so we put the tow on a line. We pulled on it but we just couldn't steer. We didn't realize why it was so hard but we found out later that we had the first Kort nozzle brought out on this coast and it was too big. It was like a huge sea anchor underneath, so big you could stand up in it. Pressure from all the water running through it caused the tow to slew from side to side. We could only make five and a half knots even when we were running light. It was really hard to steer bringing it into Vancouver. The water was so rough I had to stand outside on the winch and every time the line would come up, meaning the tug was in one swell and the towed tug in another, we had to come in on a short line through First Narrows. Regulations said that in this kind of situation we could not have a tow line over 200 feet long. So I had to pull a little bit of the brake off so it wouldn't pull the winch itself off. It was a real wild night, a heck of a way to come home for Christmas.

Another Christmas, about 1948, we came in on the *G.H. French* and the hulk of the tug *Peerless* was sitting at Coyle's dock. They'd taken all of the machinery and metal out of it. Doug Coyle told us to take it up to Centre Bay on Gambier Island and sink it. So we towed it up to Centre Bay and opened the seacocks but without the weight of all of its steel, it didn't want to sink. And we couldn't go home for Christmas until it sank. So I suggested to the skipper that we set it on fire. He said to go ahead. I went on board and there were still the bunks in there with the old mattresses. I poured some coal oil onto one of the mattresses and lit a match to it. That really gave me a lot of respect for people who didn't want you to smoke on tugs because I just walked out of the door and went over to the one line that we had attached from the *G.H. French* to the *Peerless*. By the time I got that one line off and jumped aboard our tug, the heat was really intense with the fire catching on all the years and years of painting on the *Peerless*. There was a little bit of a hole through the door and it was like a huge blowtorch, with the velocity of the heat coming out. In seven minutes there was nothing left. The bottom of the hull was water-logged and heavy and it sank when the upperworks were burnt off. When I got my own tug it was wooden and I would never allow smoking inside. If you wanted to smoke you had to go outside at the winch in the stern.

Every tug has a personality. For example, the Seaspan Mariner *was dubbed a "submarine" for the way it went through waves, not over them. It was a "wet" boat like others that were stable enough but did not rise to waves well and would hold a deckload of water. The* Seaspan Voyager *was dubbed "tender" for its quick-rolling tendency. It would roll into the trough of a wave and hang there before righting, throwing the crew off their feet if they weren't careful.*

Former towboater and part-time tour boat skipper, **Captain Bob McCoy**, *recalls a mechanical quirk that dogged a particular tug:*

I had some scary things happen, especially when I was on the *Seaspan Wave*. She had this habit of going full astern, just like that. She had what they call a controllable pitch wheel, a CP wheel. What would happen was that one of the servo pumps, that has something to do with the hydraulics, would break down in the engine room and there was a little space of time before the other one cut in automatically. So during that period the propeller would reverse its pitch. And, of course, when the second pump cut in you were going full astern. This happened to me off Cape Mudge with a paper barge and a rail barge. I was just writing the time in the logbook and the deckhand said, "She's not steering." And just then, bump, she backed into the first barge. The tug spun around and lay across the bow of the paper barge, the rail barge came down with the tide and tore a big hole in the tug's steel bulwarks. The engineer got her going again and I got the barges into Duncan Bay. I contacted Seaspan and told them that this thing had gone full astern on me again. This was the third time it happened.

A previous time I was at Van Anda on Texada Island at the lime rock loading dock, and the barge was a little longer than what the loader could reach. I asked the mate if he had handled this type of boat before and he said, "Oh, yes." I was on hours of rest, so I told him to slide the barge ahead about 30 feet for them and get the other deckhand out so that there would be two guys to help him. I woke up to a terrible crash. The boat was lying on its side. The door flew open. The deckhand comes in and says, "We're on the rocks. You've gotta get up." So I got up. What had happened, the mate had put the throttle ahead and she started to back on him and ended up right on the rocks. By this time, of course, she'd bounced off the beach. There was only a little breeze blowing and she drifted over to the barge. The propeller was just shreds and the rudder was jammed over. I had to wait for a tow down to Vancouver. After these problems they ran all the time with the two servo pumps on, so if one went, the other would still be running. The *Seaspan Breeze* had the same set up and she did the same thing several times but the *Wave* was very bad for it.

I was securing a barge up again at Van Anda on Texada Island. I put the barge alongside and the deckhand picked the line up from the dock. He let my towing bridles go so that I could go around and push the barge into position. I started to move forward but was moored to the beach by my starboard propeller. There was a big poly tie-up line that used to run from the beach. Someone had dumped it in the water. Nightime, I didn't see it; I went astern and picked this darn thing up. It was in my Kort nozzle. I was sitting there with my stern about 15 feet off the beach. I took a chance and went full ahead on the other engine and I broke the line. I pulled out and I gave the engine a cou-

ple of little kicks, and this great big bundle of poly rope came up. I couldn't leave it just drifting around, so I took it out. Of all the weird things to happen. You tie up a barge and find yourself tied to the beach. Towboating can go from humdrum to nerve-racking, but all in all it's a dandy job.

The tug *Queen* alongside a salvage scow after encountering a spot of trouble. The handsome old steamer was built in 1914 in New Westminster and ended her years as a liveaboard before coming to the end of the line in 1993.

CHAPTER 5

Rescues and Salvages

On the seemingly uneventful morning of March 6, 1945, the *Green Hill Park*, a 10,700-ton freighter, was loading at Pier B in Burrard Inlet. Longshoremen were stowing a cargo of newsprint, chemicals, distress signals, food and spare parts. At the nearby BA Oil dock, skipper Cyril Andrews and his crewman, Cec Phillips, were waiting for orders on the Gulf of Georgia Towing Company tug *Cuprite*. Just before noon the call came through.

Smoke and flames billow from the *Green Hill Park* after three explosions ripped through her on March 6, 1945, while she was tied to Pier B on Burrard Inlet's south shore. Tugs towed the flaming freighter into the outer harbour. VMM

Capt. Cyril Andrews, ca.1957.
CYRIL ANDREWS COLLECTION

Opposite: A Christmas tie-up
including the RFM and *Sea Wave*
at Vancouver Harbour
Commission wharf, December
24, 1934. Look closely and you'll
notice trees tied to the masts.
CVA, WALTER E. FROST

Captain Andrews had a passion for ships since he was a child. "I was just crazy to go to sea. I don't know why. I hadn't been on boats or anything," he would later recall. He began his career on the CPR ship Princess Charlotte *in 1929, then worked on a sternwheeler in the Yukon. He signed on as crewman on tugs, learned well, and had become a respected skipper.*

The longshoremen finished loading from one side and signalled to Captain Andrews that they needed to have a scow that was tied alongside the ship turned so they could reach the rest of the lumber. What happened in the next few minutes changed the rest of Captain Andrews' life.

We went in there and I had the deckhand letting go the lines off the scow. We were touching it and up against the *Green Hill Park*—and she blew. It sounded like a shot out of hell. When I saw the first explosion go straight up, it blew the hatchtender with it. He went as high as the Marine Building and landed back on the deck. There were three blasts altogether and they blew me out of the wheelhouse every time. I had to be in close because there were men in the water and I had to get them out. The lumber barge was on fire, roaring. We backed away from it and started pulling people out of the water. It was strange because we didn't know who they were. Men were climbing down ropes dangling from the ship's side but were dropping like grapes from a vine at each explosion. I backed up to the dock and let the men off that we'd pulled from the water. A newspaper photographer jumped on board and went out with us as we looked for more survivors.

Debris was raining on buildings and streets. Pickles from the cargo fell like green hail. Hundreds of windows shattered in buildings from the waterfront to Georgia Street. **Captain Andrews:**

We finally got the *Green Hill Park* away from the dock. Some people on the wharf had let the lines go. In the midst of the smoke and flames we pushed and pulled, then a bunch of boats came in to help. George Grey on the *Sumas* took the burning scow out into the middle of the harbour so we could get at the flaming ship. We got her pushed out a little bit and turned her around. The *RFM*, a big tug, went in and put a line on her and started towing her out. We headed out of the harbour. She was turning this way and that and I was right alongside of her, pushing on her portside trying to keep her straight. We tried to put her on the beach where Vancouver Wharves are now, in North Vancouver, but the tide washed her off. She was burning furiously. I said to my deckhand, "I don't know if she's going to blow again." We

were only about 15 feet from her. "Well," he said, "maybe we won't know this time if she blows." They tried to stop us from pushing her under Lions Gate Bridge in case she blew and destroyed the bridge, never mind about us. The bridge controller was attempting to divert water traffic by shouting through his megaphone but no one could hear him. We finally got her up on the beach at Siwash Rock and three fireboats pumped 35 feet of water in her over the next three days and nights to get the fire out.

Afterwards Gulf of Georgia Towing provided the official boat for investigations. We were around there for about a week, with a representative from the underwriter firm Lloyd's of London. Every time a body was found he and I had to go up on board to verify its location. It wasn't a very nice job. In one place a guy had tried to climb a ladder inside and he got caught. His arms were burnt off at his elbows, his legs were burnt off at his knees and his head was burnt off. He was hung on the ladder under his armpits.

Later that month I began having severe dizzy spells and collapsing. I hadn't known I had a concussion from being blown out of the wheelhouse. So the company took me off the tugs and I worked for the Towboat Owners' Association that had a hiring hall of their own called the Towboat Employment Agency at 220 Alexander Street in Vancouver. I couldn't work on a boat but I needed employment. I was in and out of the hospital so many times and they were really trying to do something for me. I felt like I saw every doctor in the country. I was fed up with it. My head hurt so much. Everything would go black in front of me. One doctor told me it was all in my mind. An Air Force doctor took me on and worked with me for years and eventually got me halfway straightened out. They finally found out that my pituitary gland had been squashed by the explosion. I had to have an injection every day of my life for several years. I finally felt better.

The federal government investigated the Green Hill Park *disaster and, based on available evidence, found that the explosion was caused by "improper*

stowage of combustible, dangerous and explosive material in No. 3 'tween decks and ignition thereof by a lighted match." The commission's assumption was confirmed years later by a deathbed confession. A longshoreman had dropped a match while he and several others were broaching barrels of overproof whiskey in the ship's darkened hold. The whiskey caught fire and flares stowed on top of the barrels ignited. An unstoppable inferno ensued.

Six longshoremen and two crew died in the explosion, 19 men were injured and flying glass hurt dozens of office workers.

In December 1953, another disaster actually changed the course of search and rescue on the BC coast and Captain Andrews again was involved. The tug C.P. Yorke was running light up the coast one night. "The crew members were all good friends of ours," Captain Andrews

C.P. Yorke November 1952 — Entering Vancouver Harbour, First Narrows. In December of the following year, six men drowned when she collided with Tattenham Shoal, near Secret Cove, capsized and sank. This catastrophe became a catalyst for the creation of Search and Rescue. VMM

recalled. "We'd see them in the office regularly. Every time a crew would leave they'd come into the office and say, 'Hi you guys. Just saying hello.'" Only a few hundred yards from Secret Cove, going up through Welcome Pass, the C.P. Yorke *hit Tattenham Shoal. Skipper Roy Johnson apparently wasn't concerned when the boat grounded, expecting it to float off with the tide. But when a wild southeaster came up, the waves and rocks ground a hole in the hull. The* C.P. Yorke *rolled over and sank. There were several boats nearby but in those days tugs' radios were usually tuned to music, probably Bill Ray and his Roundup. So they couldn't hear the* C.P. Yorke's *mayday.*

Captain Andrews:

The company sent me and a diver on a salvage boat up there by car to search for bodies. I had a phone in the car, one of the first ones. I told George Unwin, who was the diver, that we'd meet him in Pender Harbour. Next day we went out on the boat looking for bodies. And

H & L in 1953 off Howe Sound. The crew of the H & L spotted the C.P. Yorke's captain, one of two survivors of the accident, clutching a flashlight, unconscious but still alive. The C.P. Yorke's mayday most likely went unheard because nearby boat radios were tuned to music bands. VMM

we found six, unfortunately. The captain had been kept afloat in a life jacket but it was the middle of winter. He was found in the water by the crew of the tug *H & L* that saw the beam of a flashlight clutched in his hand. That's how they happened to find him. He was alive but unconscious. The first mate of the *H & L* dived into the water with a line. He attached it to Captain Johnson, and the tug's crew pulled them both aboard. The nurse told me at the hospital that they had a terrible time prying the flashlight out of his hand. The next day people living along the coast found the engineer on shore. He had floated 10 miles on the hull of an overturned lifeboat. He was freezing cold but came through all right. The rest died. We got the bodies and the boat. It was raised from about 80 feet of water by Straits Towing and was running again after a complete overhaul. This catastrophe, in my mind, is what started Search and Rescue. In those days the government wasn't willing to establish Coast Guard on the coast.

Attempting to salvage the tug-boat *Ella McKenzie*, April 28, 1939, Vancouver, BC. CVA

I thought, It's so ridiculous, all the boats have radios on them but most of the crews are tuned to a music band and can't hear a mayday call. So I went to see my board of directors, who were elected every year from the towboat companies, and told them I'd like to take all those radio bands with music on them out of the wheelhouses so the crews couldn't listen to music there, and put a radio in the galley for amusement. In the wheelhouse the radios would be tuned to 2,182 kilocycles, the distress frequency. The directors thought that was a good idea, so the board sent out messages to all the companies about what they were going to do. And they did it in April 1954. Then we had framed notices made up for all the tugs with what to do in case of emergency and the steps to go through. Printed across the bottom was this: "The life you save may be your own."

This marine rescue arm, as it was called informally (later the Rescue Co-ordination Centre), worked closely with the RCAF at their Jericho base in Vancouver. Combined air and sea rescue services could be called on when necessary. Captain Andrews was still working out of the towboat office but could not receive direct calls from the boats. Their mayday calls would go out to any government radio station that could pick them up, who then relayed them to Andrews on the radio telephone in the office, his car or his home. He then contacted any vessels in the vicinity of the accident and the captain of one of them was appointed search master. Andrews was on call 24 hours a day and was not comfortable with the fact that the boats could not contact him directly. Finally Captain Andrews came up with a solution:

I used to go down to Second Narrows bridge on my day off and sit and chew the fat with the boys while they were working. I thought, "Their radio is only five watts, but why can't we use

that?" So they got permission from their office for me to use it. But the government representative refused: "You cannot use that radio, period!" I said, "I'm damn well going to use it." He said, "I'm ordering you." But I told him I was going to use it anyway. After all, men's lives were at stake. He said it wouldn't reach up the coast but I asked him how come I could speak to the Coast Guard in Alaska on it. There was a write-up in the paper about the feud. Finally I asked him what if someone jumped off the bridge or fell off a boat. Would I have to use a special lifebuoy to throw to that man in the water because we couldn't use your lifebuoys? There was a regular war going on but I kept using the radio. Of course the towboat owners were behind me. The Second Narrows bridge radio was a monitoring station and listening all the time. If something went wrong they phoned my office

When the *Unimak* sank in 1960 all four aboard were killed, the last trapped in an air pocket and banging on the hull as would-be rescuers looked on helplessly. PHOTO COURTESY UBC LIBRARY RARE BOOKS AND SPECIAL COLLECTIONS, FISHERMEN PUBLISHING SOCIETY.

right away and I would jump in my car and boil on down to the bridge and use their station. Finally the rescue service got going so well that they formed a committee of companies involved. There was one representative each from the towboat owners, the pilotage, the CPR, Union Steamships, the Fishing Vessels Association, the CNR, Northland Navigation, and me. They all agreed that if we needed any of their boats I had the authority to take them and use them, it didn't matter for how long, and for no cost. Nobody paid anything.

In one instance I held up a CPR boat one day in 1960 when we were trying to rescue someone in an upturned boat. God, it was rough. The *Unimak*, a big fish boat, had hit a scow at night near Sechelt and rolled over. Someone was banging from inside the hull. I brought in the CPR ship *Princess of Vancouver*, on its way from Nanaimo to Vancouver loaded with passengers, to make a breakwater beside the fish boat so we would be able to get the guy out. We had quite a

Following its tragic accident off Gower Point in 1960, the *Unimak* was repaired and relaunched. PHOTO COURTESY UBC LIBRARY RARE BOOKS AND SPECIAL COLLECTIONS, FISHERMEN PUBLISHING SOCIETY.

dilemma. We couldn't cut a hole in the bottom of the boat or it would go down as soon as the air came out. The only thing we could do was hope to hold it up and get a diver to go inside, a pretty risky move. The guy inside kept hammering away. It was a horrible feeling. The water was getting rougher all the time. The guys tried to string tow lines between two tugboats and under the fish packer to hold it up, then we could run it ashore and cut a hole in the bottom. Of course we would still be taking the chance of hitting the fuel tanks, or steel plates. One of the rescue boats, the *Brentwood*, had a mast and derrick and we hooked that up to the *Unimak*. It was so heavy that the weight tore the *Brentwood*'s mast out. All of a sudden the fish boat righted itself, then went down. We found out later that two men inside, another man and a girl all drowned. That would have been a horrible death—in the dark—terrible. But what else could we have done? The CPR ship left then and proceeded to Vancouver. We had held up the transcontinental train for about six hours because they were waiting for the passengers. That was all okay.

We later went to the insurance companies and asked them what they were going to do to help us with our rescue efforts. They said, "If you go to a rescue, first save the lives. But if one of your tugs salvages the boat and tows it into Vancouver, we'll give you double the daily rate of the boat that's towing it." The rate depended on the horsepower of the tug. For instance if it had 1,500 horsepower they charged $1,500 an hour. But the insurance company cut down their insurance

The *Unimak* revival was short lived. Not long after it was raised in Sechelt, it collided with a tanker off Prince Rupert and went down for good. PHOTO COURTESY UBC LIBRARY RARE BOOKS AND SPECIAL COLLECTIONS, FISHERMEN PUBLISHING SOCIETY.

fees for those hours the guys were working on a salvage. Paying half of it was a good deal.

The American Coast Guard liked it so much they came up here to see how we worked and we met with them once a month. We worked all over the province, even the lakes. If you were in distress you would switch to 2,182 kilocycles and call "mayday, mayday, mayday." We had all the lighthouses on the same frequency. That's how it started and it got so big that they decided I shouldn't be in the towboat office, I should be in an office of my own. In the spring of 1956, the Department of Transport granted $10,000 toward my salary and some other expenses and I was moved to an office at the Air Force base at Jericho. It was a highly secure building because it was the end of the radar line and was guarded. My past and my relatives had to be checked. I still hold the pass for it. It was a little awkward in a way because the Air Force didn't like a beastly civilian ordering them around. But I never really ordered them around. I was marine advisor to the Air Force. Then we went to the government to ask for marine telephones so I could talk to the boats to direct what was going on. They had a five-watt government station at Point Grey, so they hooked a line from that into my office, and when something happened I could talk to all the boats and the Air Force. It was so nice because as soon as we had an emergency, I'd switch over to the 2,366 frequency that all of the tugs talked to each other on and say, "Hello the ships. Hello the ships. Hello the ships. This is Search and Rescue calling. This is a mayday call." They'd all answer back. They were always rude to me of course. On the waterfront you're always rude to each other. If you're not, there's something wrong. Jack Fish was a mate on the *Kenora.* I'd be on the air calling the ships and Jack Fish would call back, "We're out here, Curly [Andrews is bald]. What do you want us to do?" They'd give me their positions and I'd check them on my huge chart.

The Air Force boys were interested in plane rescues but with me there they were also involved in marine rescues. No helicopters were used, just seaplanes or wheeled aircraft. They would throw over lifesaving equipment or lower a line and winch the people up. They did a very good job. The only trouble with the Air Force was that they had an hour's standby. You had to give them an hour's notice. I told the Air Force that was wrong. You can't expect a guy to hold his breath for an hour. We found out from the doctors how long a guy could live in the water. They gave him at the best 30 minutes. So they brought the Air Force at Comox into it and they had a standby plane there at all times. The Air Force was always the one that spoke to the planes.

Opposite; Two boys get a closer look at the *Unimak* as it is beached at Davis Bay, August 7, 1960, more than a week after it sank off Gower Point. PHOTO COURTESY UBC LIBRARY RARE BOOKS AND SPECIAL COLLECTIONS, FISHERMEN PUBLISHING SOCIETY.

When we got our boats lined up we always appointed a search master. He took the orders from me, although I never ordered, I always asked, "Can you help?" I arranged for a moving line of boats ahead and the Air Force would drop flares. L & K Lumber in North Vancouver gave us their airplane to use if we needed it. Larry and George Lyttle said I could have that plane any time I wanted, with a pilot.

One highlight of Captain Andrews' rescue efforts involved the disappearance of five men on the Hilunga, *an 82-foot federal works department vessel. Captain Herbert Dale-Johnson had radioed at 2:30 a.m. in a raging blizzard in February 1956: "I'm going to have to abandon ship. She's breaking up." He gave their location as Cape St. James, the southern point of the Queen Charlotte Islands. After one mayday call their radio was swamped. The Air Force sent planes out looking for any sign of the boat or the men, but after two days found nothing.*

A Cates tug and the seine boat *New Venture* as they remove the net from a sunken seine boat.
UBC LIBRARY RARE BOOK AND SPECIAL COLLECTIONS, FISHERMEN PUBLISHING SOCIETY

Captain Andrews:

I put out a call to any ship that had seen the *Hilunga*. The closest I could come was the report that one boat phoned in saying that he had seen it just about at the top end of Vancouver Island and gave the day and the time. We worked out where that was, and I could calculate the speed of the *Hilunga* from the time it was seen to the time the captain got the distress out, the state of the tide and the weather, and there was no possible way she could be near Cape St. James. I drew an arc on the chart. If he had been on the portside of the arc he would have been in wide open seas. So he had to have been on the starboard side. I drew a mark across there and said there it is, on Aristazabal Island, south of the Queen Charlottes. When the Air Force went up the next day, there they were, on Aristazabal Island, waving from the rocks on the beach. The tug *Sea Monarch* picked them up that afternoon and they were transferred to a Canso rescue aircraft on the lee side of the island. It was very nice to get thank-you letters from the crew's wives. The *Hilunga* is still sailing. They brought her down to Vancouver and put a new bottom in her.

After seven years of successful service by the marine rescue arm, West Coast marine search and rescue was taken over by the federal government's Department of Transportation, which established the Canadian Coast Guard.

Captain Keast *and* **Captain Cyril Andrews** *were both present at the July 1960 sinking of the* Unimak. *Keast was also involved in the boat's salvage:*

Captain Howie Keast:

"We came across the gulf one night from Gabriola Island on the *Jean L.*, and we crossed over

Captain Andrews and the search and rescue team did enjoy some light moments during their serious searches. One day he requested assistance from some naval vessels in a search area. They radioed their position to the rescue team, who had difficulty interpreting it. "I finally sent a message to Victoria requesting confirmation of the latitude and longitude sent to us," Andrews recalls. "They agreed that it was correct. So I sent them a return message: 'Please confirm that the *Restigouche* is in Abbotsford.'"

Capt. Howie Keast, ca. 1978.

Though boom and barge towing became the main work of tugs, early tugs spent much of their time pulling sailing ships in and out of port. Here the *Sea Monarch* tows a tall ship past the mouth of Capilano River, Vancouver, 1920. VMM

to [Cape] Roger Curtis. During our crossing we came across a fishing vessel heading for Vancouver, towing a reefer barge that carried canned fish and things like that, loaded up-coast. Just east of Gower Point, the vessel towing the barge had gotten into an accident with a fishing vessel called the *Unimak* that had crossed the stern of the tow vessel in front of the barge. Consequently the towline flipped the fishing vessel over, and it then caught up on the bridle gear. You can imagine the position that the skipper of the towing vessel was in. What do you do? Do you slow down? If you slow down it might sink. If you keep going you might hold it up. It was a difficult situation and a hard decision to make.

As we were getting in past Roger Curtis with our log tow, a westerly wind had started coming up with a swell. There were several vessels including the CPR vessel *Princess of Vancouver* to give some

assistance. Several tugs were in the vicinity and came to give a hand, but to no avail. These people in the boat were trapped upside down and had no way of knowing which way the boat was because of blackness. If the rescuers tried to cut a hole in the boat with a chain saw there was some chance that the vessel might sink because the air inside would escape. So with the swell, and increasing westerly wind, the vessel was getting lower in the water. You couldn't beach it properly because of all the problems with the masts, stay wires and so forth. Consequently the vessel sank, but had drifted far west of Gower Point towards White Islets. A diver named Frank Wright went down and tried to see if there was anything he could do. He found a girl but she was already drowned. The vessel took two men down, and there was little they could do in that situation.

A few weeks later we took on the job of salvaging the *Unimak*. We used a barge with a logging donkey from L & K Lumber, a Caterpillar and an arch that they used for hauling logs out of the woods. The grappling gear involved the barge, assisted by the *Kathy L.* and our tug, the *Jean L.* We had a big sweeping line going from the barge to our tug, and we dragged along the bottom in a large loop. When we thought that we had hold of something, we'd use what we called a haulback line attached to a logging block or shiv, which would tighten up the loop and go around the vessel or whatever we had hold of on the bottom. Then we would haul up what was attached. Eventually we found the *Unimak*, but we didn't know what we had ahold of. So we brought it up and the RCMP patrol vessel gave us a hand with their depth-sounder to show us the best way to get in to the beach. While we were holding this vessel just below the surface of the water, we used an inch-

and-an-eighth cable, which was rubbing on the angle iron on the barge's bumper. The steel stranded the cable and it broke. Back down goes the vessel. It was so heavy. The wood was just saturated, impregnated with water, and it was down 450 feet, very deep to find without using electronics. We checked the amount of water pressure later with someone at UBC who said it was 198 pounds per square inch, so you can imagine the pressure that was on it. When we did get ahold of it the first time a lot of the penboards floated to the surface. They're eight feet long, six or eight inches wide, two inches thick and used for making various pens for fish in the hole of the fish boat, and they were just barely floating. A propane tank came flying up from the bottom and blew off all the propane, and gallon cans came up that were squished, crushed together. There was a lot of pressure there.

So after losing the boat, and trying for the second time, we

The *La Pointe* tows a chip scow. This 805-horsepower tug was purchased by Vancouver Tugboat Company in 1933. If a tug is forced to slow down or stop unexpectedly it is in peril of being overridden by its own tow. Here, the tow line is very short to give more control of the tow but this also increases the chances of being overtaken by the massive scow. VMM rearranged our grappling gear, and shortened up the line to the logging donkey to give us a better purchase on the winch. We caught the boat again, and this time we brought it up and held it. The sweeping line must have come up over its stern and the loop tightened on the drag boards cabled to the deck. They are used on fishing boats to drag along the bottom, attached to the fishing nets that are above and behind them. We were worried that the boards would come loose. If our line had come up over the bow, it would have slipped off over the stay lines. We took it in to Davis Bay at Sechelt, beached it, and waited for higher water to float it further in. In the meantime we got some barrels from the Chevron at Sechelt and put them in the fishing hole of the vessel. They helped to give it more buoyancy at the next high water. When the tide came in we moved it in a little further and when the tide went down the RCMP were there to get the bodies out. This was a Sunday morning, and the priest came down and told me that we had a bigger congregation than he did at the church. We patched the boat up and towed it into the shipyard at Coal Harbour. It was repaired and went back to sea again. However, the last I heard of that vessel was that it was hit by an Imperial Oil tanker up off of Prince Rupert and went down with no loss of life. But the boat went down and never came up again.

I still have a shotgun and a lifebuoy as mementos from the *Unimak*. The shotgun today is rusty, I would never use it, but it is a treasure. We found out later that the *Unimak* was one of the deepest wrecks on the coast brought up to the surface without electronics to aid in locating.

Towboaters performed their dangerous rescue and salvage efforts with little public fanfare, which suited them just fine. But the gratitude of fellow mariners was a cherished keepsake; **Captain Keast** *recalls one such occasion:*

On a gale-ridden day approximately 1960, on the *Jean L.,* we tied up with a log tow to what we know as Southeast Rock, best known as Trail Islands off Sechelt. In those days there was no traffic centre as there is now. The Cape Lazo lightkeeper, with his deep, husky voice, gave the weather forecasts in the area, plus messages to the various vessels. I received a call from Cape Lazo that there was a fishing vessel aground at Welcome Point, just east of Welcome Pass. The southeast wind was blustering at 50 knots with gusts to 60. There was a heavy sea running.

We took off and arrived at what tugboat skippers know as Welcome
Point, known on the chart as Precision Point. On arrival all we saw was
the gillnet vessel aground and the sea was breaking over the whole
boat. We wondered how any human could possibly live through that.
We tried to manoeuvre as close as possible but there was still no one
visible on board. Then with the binoculars we saw a man in the door-
way of the fishing vessel. This was getting dangerous for us because to
stay in position with the wind and the sea would put us in jeopardy,
too. I called RCC [Rescue Co-ordination Centre] and told them the
situation. They asked what I would suggest, and my answer was a helicopter, as soon as possible. It was there so fast I couldn't believe it.
They had their hands full and deserved every credit for what they did.
This person aboard the fishing vessel didn't want to leave it. I assume
this could have been his home. However he was taken off and transported to Vancouver General Hospital. A *Province* reporter called me

Capt. Howie Keast at controls of
the *Lawrence L.* after the Home
Oil fuel barge explosion in Coal
Harbour, 1974. Crewmembers
man fire hoses on the aft deck
and the Vancouver fireboat is at
right rear. HOWIE KEAST COLLECTION

on the radio telephone, telling me what a good job we had done but I told him the members of the helicopter crew were the real rescuers. He said the fisherman was fine and that he would never forget the green and white tug that saved his life.

On January 4, 1974, we were at the Lyttle Brothers dock at the foot of Philip in North Vancouver. We had just finished an engine overhaul and the engines had started. We were warming them up in order to tune the engines later on. While we were doing this there was a huge explosion out on the water. There was a workshop at the end of the dock with plastic siding and some of this was really shaking from the blast. We didn't know what had happened until we looked over near Brockton Point and saw all this black smoke. I had a good idea then what had happened, being familiar with the harbour and knowing about the gas barges tied up at the entrance to Coal Harbour. I talked it over with the mechanics and we decided to go and see if we could be of any assistance. The rest of the crew was Raymond Smart, Ron Lowe and assistant skipper Ken Arnison. When we got over there on the *Lawrence L.*, the Home Oil barge was just an exploding, blazing inferno. You couldn't get near it, it was so hot. We did see a small yacht tied up alongside and it was on fire too. We got on the lee side so the heat and flames were blowing away from us. Captain Dan Williams, skipper of the *Seaspan Venture* was nearby, and seeing that the barge was still attached to the pilings, he rammed his vessel into the burning hulk and ripped out the mooring chains. There were several other tugs there, plus the fireboat with two L & K tugs helping it. The barge started to drift toward the Esso barge, which could have caused another devastating explosion. The Esso barge was about three times the capacity of the Home Oil barge. However we manoeuvred around and managed to get hold of the flaming barge with a two-inch poly line. We used our hoses with a spray nozzle trying to keep the crew cooled off so they could get the line on the barge's deck. We took a pull on the line but before we could get moving the line was burnt and broke, so we used our heavy deep-sea gear. It was very difficult to get the tow line onto the barge and we put it onto a rake timber which was exposed with the deck having burned away. We started to move the barge but only just in time because it was really close to the Esso barge where the heat had broken windows and bubbled the paint, but we managed to get it out of there just in the nick of time—seconds would have made all the difference in the world. We took it out to the middle of the harbour, where we began to have problems on board. The fireboat had used up all of its foam and was now spraying water on the fire, with one tug on each side to keep it in position. It had come too close to us and its monitor hit our floodlights on the mast's yardarm and they fell to the deck, causing a short and fire on the switchboard down in the engine room. The engineer rushed below and pulled a switch to isolate the short circuit. We managed to get the fire out but then our radios went out and we had no communication. With our radio cut off I couldn't receive any orders over the air for about 20 minutes. The harbour master, other tugs and fire boat couldn't reach us to give directions. So we did what we thought was best. Eventually radio power was restored.

We were then asked where we were taking the barge and I suggested to the North Shore, or the middle of the harbour or whatever, as long as it was away from habitation because it was still exploding. Finally it was agreed that we would take it to the Fullerton site on the North Shore, east of Seaspan today, where it was corralled with boomsticks. The North Vancouver District fire department was there when we arrived and they played their hoses on the fire. It took 12 hours to burn itself out.

Captain Maynard:

We were coming down the coast on a little tug called the *Leslie Ann,* which was about 50 feet in length. It was really miserable weather, southeast winds, storm forecast. We pulled into Lund for the night. We were just sitting down to have some supper, and after that we were going to go up to the pub and have a few beer, because what else are you going to do in a place like Lund? The owner of the store, Roy Edmundson, came down and said, "Hey, there's a boat in trouble between here and Ragged Islands. Could you go up and have a look?" Naturally, we went out. It was blowing 60 or 70 knots. Before we left I got the crew to rig a lifeline from the stern of the tug up to the towing winch, so they'd have something to hang onto while they were trying to rescue people. We found about a 16-foot plywood boat with four people in it and an engine that wouldn't run. We managed to get them aboard with quite a bit of difficulty. The waves were going across our deck. We got close enough that one of the boys could get hold of the small boat with a pike pole and pull it to us. Then we hauled them out of the boat but there was no way to put a decent line on it. There was a half-inch to three-quarter-inch line on the bow of the boat that we got hold of and hooked onto a polyprop line of our own. Before we started out for Lund I asked the people we'd got on board whose boat

The *Sudbury*'s mate, Jimmy Talbott, fires the rocket gun toward the *Makedonia*, launching a line over the freighter's bulwarks. The *Sudbury* made headlines around the world for this dramatic 1955 rescue.
SEASPAN INTERNATIONAL

it was. One fellow said it was his. I said, "Well, I'm telling you that I hope it's insured. We're going to Lund, and I'm not looking back 'til we get there. It's too dangerous to be playing around trying to rescue something like that." He said, "That's fine. It's insured. I'm glad to be alive." So we get to Lund and the boat was still there. We drank plenty of beer that night and we didn't have to pay for it.

Later on that same trip we were in Howe Sound to pick up a tow and take it to the Fraser River and there was a call put out that a deep-sea ship had broken down three miles off Cape Roger Curtis on Bowen Island. It was a new 12,000-ton general cargo ship named the *Sea Tide*, only three weeks old and on its maiden voyage. It was blowing 40 to 50 knots westerly and he was drifting shoreward. So we went out and towed him into English Bay.

As a crewman on deep-sea vessels, **Captain Aage Fransvaag** *had learned the importance of the conventions that are often referred to as the code of the sea:*

A message had come to the Search and Rescue in Victoria. There was a commercial fish boat, American, broken down off Tofino down the line from Estevan. Captain Don Chatt got permission to be dismissed from the standby job we were on there. We ran down to try and get a line off the broken-down fish boat and managed to do it but the captain hurt himself pretty badly. He fell with his legs between the stepladder from the wheelhouse down to the boat deck but he just carried on. As crew we were laying down on the aft deck and we finally got a line onto this boat and towed it back to Moyeha Bay in Nootka Sound and tied it up. I kind of waited for one of the crew from the fish boat to come over to Captain Chatt to say thank you. One of their guys had broken his arm and hurt his nose. But not a soul came. By the morning I was burning, I was so angry. So I went over to talk to these guys. They all spoke Norwegian, as I do, and were from Ballard, Washington. I told them that according to the code of the sea it would be very nice if they would go and extend their thanks to our skipper for a job well done. I told them I meant it. They finally did. But in the next few months everything was pacified because our company claimed salvage and as crew members we got a bit of salvage money too. Not very much—a couple of hundred dollars. But that was enough. It was such an alien attitude among sailors. Maybe they were too tired to even think about it. Just glad to be alive.

Captain MacPherson *remembers that the challenges of working on the Fraser River were compounded when someone made a mistake:*

On one trip on the Fraser River we were dropping a scow down through the BC Hydro bridge immediately west of Oak Street, and I had called Bridge Towing for an assist. I was dropping the barge backwards through the bridge opening as rules dictated at freshet time, meaning that the tug was heading upriver into a very fast current, so that I had to use a lot of throttle to maintain a slow speed, dropping the barge down gently. The prop wash and the river current caused a boiling swell behind the barge. For some unknown reason the skipper of the Bridge Towing tug, the *Chugaway*, tried to put a line on the barge, which he never should have done. I had no way of knowing what was going on. I didn't hear from him on the radio, so I didn't know the tug had rolled over on its beam and thrown him off. I saw the bridge tender was panicking trying to get my attention. The *Chugaway* deckhand was climbing up on top of the load and yelled, "The skipper's in the water!" I immediately dropped my bridles because it was more important to try and get him. I lowered the mast to go under the fixed span and just let the barge drift. The tug had righted itself but was going around in circles. We then saw him hanging on to one of the tug's fenders. The danger was going alongside and crushing him. We had to shut the props off on his tug before he went under. The deck-hand jumped aboard, pulled it into neutral, grabbed the skipper and hauled him up on deck. Another tug came up the river and pulled alongside. They lifted him onto their tug and we went running back to catch our barge that was drifting down the centre arm. We were afraid it would take out the airport bridge. We just caught it. We were so busy during all this that it wasn't really exciting. You don't really think about it all until later. We got to Oak Street for a crew change and I drove to the skipper's house on the way home. It really hit me when we got to his place and saw two or three little kids running around. We had a drink together. I think I was more upset then than we were in action. The only thing that happened to him was that he lost his glasses.

Vancouver Tugboat's *La Pointe* on trials after being refitted. One of the first steel boats used for major tugboat work, it was originally the *Kingsway*, an early-1900s North Sea fishing trawler. Capt. Alan Stanley recalls an evening in September of 1965 when the *La Pointe* saved the lives of four teenagers. DM

Captain Alan Stanley *was raised fishing with his father at Rivers Inlet and has seen numerous mishaps on the water:*

One evening, sometime about 1965, we were coming up past the Sand Heads off the mouth of the Fraser River, heading to Vancouver on the *La Pointe* with a chip barge. It had just got dark and we saw this dim little light flashing out on the water. So we went over to investigate and put a searchlight on where this light was shining. We could see figures on the bottom of an overturned

powerboat. So we went over and took aboard four young people in their teens and twenties. They had been coming over from Vancouver Island to head up the Fraser River and had hit a deadhead which capsized the boat. These young men and women were just hanging on for their lives to the bottom of their overturned craft. There was hardly more than the size of a tabletop showing above the water. One of the girls told me that when the boat was going over, she had to decide whether to grab her purse or a flashlight. She chose the flashlight. That was the flashing light that we had seen. The pilot boat came out of Steveston and picked up the kids and took them in and also towed the small vessel into the river as well. We just continued on. You know, it's really a small world because when I got home I phoned my wife,

Dawn, and told her that we'd picked up these four kids in the water. A few days later we found out that the girl with the flashlight was the niece of a very good friend of ours.

Captain Baese:

We had tied up in Nugent Sound and had started to come down with a tow through Schooner Pass when we got a mayday from a boat off of Allison Harbour. This fellow worked at the Interfor logging camp about 60 miles from the head of Seymour Inlet. He lived in Port Hardy and would come up and work his 10 days, then he'd go home for four days. He had this little pleasure boat and he'd waved at us as he was going through. He got into trouble at the rocks off of Allison Harbour. There was a pretty big swell out there. He called on the radio and asked if there was any way we could get him some help out there because the boat was sinking. I told him to hold on as long as he could and I would phone the logging camp and ask them to come out with their helicopter as I was a third of the way down Allison Pass with a log tow. I phoned and told them that the guy was out there and his boat was sinking. Before they got there his boat had sunk and he'd got out on

The cruise ship *Meteor* caught fire May 17, 1971. As she slumps to starboard, a coast guard boat attempts to extinguish the lethal fire, while Seaspan tugs, *Le Beau* and *La Garde* assist. The *Sudbury II* eventually came to the rescue, but not before 32 of the *Meteor's* crewmembers were killed in the fire. SEASPAN INTERNATIONAL

the rocks. It was low tide but it was coming in. A helicopter from the camp came down and plucked him off that rock just before the tide was too high. If it had been a half-hour later, he'd have been washed off that rock in the swell.

Captain Bull *had 20 years of sea experience when he was asked to salvage the loaded log barge* Forest Prince, *which had gone up on Long Beach in 1968:*

We went in on the *Sudbury II* and because of the way the seas were—it was winter time—I said I couldn't get in any closer than a mile, so send us a mile of line. They said okay, go into Bamfield and wait. We did and tied up at the cable station and waited about five days or a week. They came up with a nine-inch circumference Sampson braid with a thimble on each end. As it turned out, it was only 4,000 feet. They could not make it a mile. We decided to have a go at it and went back out. They'd made arrangements for a helicopter to come out to pick up the end. I took the tug in, anchored it, and the helicopter came over and picked up the end with a wire bridle on it and started off inshore with it. It was okay except that the current took the line and put a big belly in it and we ended up adding on any line we could find, including shoelaces, so we could get the bridle on the barge. We managed to do that and we started pulling at our end. To make the connection I had to pay out more anchor chain which didn't make me happy at all, not knowing where those rocks were. Eventually it all came together; we hooked up to the tow line. We paid out a little tow line to get the Sampson braid clear of the stern, and they started discharging the load on the barge. They were doing fine, the weather wasn't too bad, but when the weather forecast came on at nine o'clock that night I talked to them on the beach and told them there was a gale warning for the area and they said okay, and started just throwing the logs off. Prior to this they had been handling them pretty carefully so they wouldn't break them. The logs started flying off like matchsticks. About 11 o'clock that night they said okay, high water's coming up, be ready to go… pull! And pull we did and off came the log barge. We just headed south into the darkness then turned around and went in toward Juan de Fuca and at daylight shortened up and went into Ucluelet. The brains all came down to the dock and looked at the barge and said it looked all right, so take it into Esquimalt and look at it under water. We did and left it at the dry dock wall. That was the last time I ever saw it.

Tugboat *Fearful* alongside barge,
June 4, 1921. CVA

We were on our regular lime rock run, the beginning of January 1968, when we got a message to go out and find the *Mandoil II*, an oil tanker that had been hit in dense fog by a Japanese freighter, the *Suwaharu*, loaded with logs. The *Mandoil* had a gash 75 to 100 feet long on the starboard bow and had become a mass of flames and explosions. It was carrying 300,000 tons of light oil that had spread over the water, flaming. So we dropped the barge in Victoria and went out to find this ship. There was a US Coast Guard cutter already on the scene, so we went out and kind of teamed up with them. When we got there we found out there was a ship called the *Transoneida* there first, a jumboed T-2 tanker, and they said they had a line on board. Well, that line

stretched and stretched and stretched. Finally, I said, "Let's just go in and have a look." So I sneaked in and found that he didn't have a tow line on board, but apparently they had been on the ship and had taken the log books. I guess they were trying to make some kind of a salvage claim.

After looking things over, I decided to tow from the stern because everything forward of the bridge was wide open to the sea. I was afraid the bow would pull off. So we put the salvage crew on board using our motor lifeboat. They were five guys that we'd picked up from Island Tug's yard in Victoria. I held the tug in close to the stern of the ship and we passed them the bight of a light wire that they put around a suitable bitt. Then we hove on the wire, and the end to which we had secured our wire bridles was pulled up on the ship and secured on board. The salvage crew stayed on board that night. Even though the fire was out, something started burning back aft later, and then they wanted off. The Coast Guard cutter was still standing by, so I asked him to go in and take them off. They put a life raft over and drifted it

The *Sudbury II*, proud successor to the famed *Sudbury*. VMM

down to the ship. The salvage crew all jumped into the life raft and got back to the cutter. The next day they did the same thing again and we took our crew back onto the tug.

The wire bridles only lasted 24 to 36 hours before they parted in the chock. I was down having breakfast when I felt the tug jerk. I said, "Oh-oh, wait for the next one." Then she jerked again. The second mate came down and reported the tow line had parted so I told him to slow down, get power on deck and start heaving in the tow line. That was us disconnected. Then we went through the drill again—boat over, run crew to ship, hold tug in close, pass wire bight up and haul wire

with a short piece of two-inch chain to sit in the chocks and prevent chafing. Make fast wire. Then pass a similar wire with chain connected to the other quarter so we have a bridle to our tow line. Then bring back the salvage crew and bring on board and hoist boat. Then we got underway again. After a couple of days towing we were not making much speed so the dispatcher asked if it would help if he sent out another tug. I agreed that it would certainly help, so the *Island Monarch* appeared on the scene and again we went into our boat drill to secure the *Monarch*'s tow line and carried on to the northeast.

We were told not to cross a certain meridian of longitude until it

The Liberian tanker *Mandoil II* after a collision with a Japanese freighter left a 90-foot gash in her starboard bow, February 1968. Capt. Adrian Bull attempted salvage with the *Sudbury II*.
ADRIAN BULL COLLECTION

was decided where this vessel was going. I guess they had to satisfy a number of safety requirements. It was all figured out before we got to that longitude point, so we just kept on going, and we ended up at Muchalat Inlet at Nootka Sound. We went into the bay as far as we could go and the *Monarch* let go her tow line and went alongside the ship. She held the ship while we let go the tow line and passed up a heavy wire to which one of our salvage anchors was attached. The anchor was put over the side and we towed slowly on the wire until the tug's bow touched the bottom, then the wire was slipped and the ship's stern was anchored. There were people all over the ship then, and they dropped both ships' anchors, and we kept pulling and pulling and paying out chain.

After we brought her in and she was all secured, I went on board to have a look around. There must have been a fireball, which started at the point of impact, rolled aft and hit the bridge, then landed on the afterdeck and rolled into the after accommodation. Both lifeboats on the starboard side were useless as they had melted in the chocks. The forward bulkhead of the bridge superstructure had all the paint seared off. The fire never entered this structure though, and inside it looked brand new. On the afterdeck the valve wheels that operated the various tank valves were damaged in that the spokes on most had melted and the valve rims were lying on the deck at the base of the spindle. The after accommodation around the engine room was just a shell with only the steel remains of tables and chairs and bunks. All combustible material had gone up in smoke. She must have hit right after a meal as in the galley the dishes were stacked to dry. Inside the engine room everything looked good; the fire had gone around the outside of it but didn't go inside. According to the surveyor, the engines had been shut down properly. Everything outside of the engine room had just vanished. The accommodation inside the bridge was untouched. It was brand new, looked beautiful like you could move right in. Apparently there had been deaths but some guys did get off in the lifeboats.

Jack Daly, our diver, was part of the salvage crew that went on originally. When he had gone on board he found a canary in a bamboo cage. He brought it over to the *Sudbury II*. It sang and sang. After we left the ship and came home, we tied up at the Island Tug dock in Victoria, and he's walking down the gangway with this cage. The cage fell, it opened, and the bird flew away. Oh, he was mad.

Mandoil II stayed up in Muchalat Inlet until her oil was discharged into smaller tankers. Then *Sudbury II* and *Island Mariner* were dispatched to tow her into Esquimalt and lay her alongside the dry dock wall.

Opposite: The ocean-going tug *Sudbury II*, with a bulk cargo barge in tow. Renowned for its deep-sea rescues, the ship carried a steel-cored tow line two inches in diameter and over half a mile long. VMM

Another time we went out and picked up a former Liberty ship, the *Tainan* in December 1965. Originally built in Baltimore as *Lawrence J. Brangle* in April 1944, she was scrapped in Kaohsiung, Taiwan in 1968. She had been coming across the Pacific in ballast, which didn't really give a fair shot in bad weather because the weight of the ballast didn't take the ship down deep enough for the propeller to grip the water. It would be going up and down, fore and aft, pitching, and the engineer, poor guy, had to stand by that throttle on the main engine, and when he felt the stern lift he had to slow down to prevent the prop from spinning in air. He had to stand at this big wheel and shut the steam off to slow the engine because the prop was spinning in air, and if it was spinning too fast, when it came down and hit the water, it was like a hammer and that's when you break shafts, shear bolts or lose your propeller even. When it came down into the water the engineer had to open the engine up again to keep the ship moving. And that's what he had to do for four hours, his watch. The

In her first year with Island Tug the former British navy corvette *Sudbury* made headlines towing the disabled Greek freighter *Makedonia* 3,500 miles through a storm-swept Pacific. VMM

ballast regulations at the time were really not very fair on men or machinery. This was standard procedure. On this ship, the *Tainan*, the bolts that held one of the couplings had sheared.

We got our line on board as she had steam on deck. Then we started towing and were going along fine. We were actually towing the ship faster than she could do under her own power. I think it was the second or third day of towing when the mate said, "Oh-oh, they're signalling us." They had the Aldis lamp out. Years ago, when I was deep-sea, I could stumble through the Morse code. You had to know it for all your tickets. So between the two of us we figured out their message. We were towing the vessel too fast and her propeller was turning. Because one of the shaft couplings had let go, one or two couplings inboard from the propeller, there was a short length of shaft turning along with the prop. He was scared he was going to ruin a bearing. I remembered, years before when I was an apprentice on a ship running down the West African coast, the old man insisted on having one of the two apprentices on the wheel all the time when we were in pilotage waters. I was on the wheel listening to the pilot and the skipper talking about a runaway ship and the only way they could stop it was to trail tie-up lines from the bow, and they would hook into the propeller as it was going along and finally wind around it enough that it would stop. I told the *Tainan*'s master to do the same. But he said he would rather put someone over the side to lasso the blade. I told him he could do what he liked because he was in charge. We slowed down and waited. Finally he told us to try it again and off we went with a line wrapped around the propeller so it wouldn't turn. We took her into Esquimalt.

In the late 1960s, the SS Mills Trader, *a World War II Park ship, ran out of fuel off the coast. She was launched as the* Arlington Beach Park, *built by West Coast Shipbuilders of Vancouver and delivered February 20, 1944. Built as a tanker, she was converted to dry cargo in 1954.*

Captain Bull:

He did have a little bit of generator that gave him enough power to send very weak messages. So we sort of knew where he was, but when we went out there on the *Sudbury II* it was a dirty, dark night again. It always is. There was a blip on the radar so we figured that was him. We lined up on this blip and put her up to full speed, and damn me if the blip didn't run away from us. We never knew who it was. We could not

Sudbury II, with *Island Challenger* and *Island Commander* join forces to tow a freighter. VMM

communicate directly with the ship so at the Island Tug conference call on the radio I requested the company to ask the patrol aircraft that fly around the coast to swing by and find the ship and the tug and give us a bearing and distance. This they did and we came up to the ship just before dark.

Up 'til now the weather had been quite good but somebody had decided to make it blow a little and the sea got up. I decided to have a go at hooking up. The ship had no steam to run winches so the master divided his crew into two teams, each with a rope tackle that they would have removed from the booms. We had made up a one-legged bridle, consisting of a heavy wire, a short length of chain and another wire, which was shackled to the tow line. I had to hold the tug for about four hours right in front of the bow of the ship while the ship's crew pulled the wire on board. The ship's chain was to prevent chafing in the chock on the ship. It took them a heck of a long time to do this.

It was blowing a gale, it was raining, and I was glued to the after controls. I'd just stand there and watch and give her a little kick now and again. I wasn't physically working but doing a lot of mental straining. The guys were bringing me up coffee after coffee after coffee but not talking to me. You have to stand there, you dare not lose your concentration, but whatever you do, you don't let the crew see you sweat. It took them nearly four hours to get the wire up and connected. Anyway, we had found him and got hooked up. There was no GPS [Global Positioning System] back in those days, so I said, "Where the hell are we?" We set a course about northeast and again on the morning conference call I called the company and asked them to send out a patrol aircraft to see if they could find us. So out he came and found us. He used the Morse lamp again and told us we were so many miles and a bearing off Triangle Island at the north end of Vancouver Island. So we headed on in. We only had a wire on the ship, so I decided to go inside at Port Hardy and put a chain bridle on her. I decided then to come down the inside of Vancouver Island. We were doing fine until we got off of Campbell River. Of course it had to be at night that we did these silly things. We didn't make it out to Cape Mudge before the tide changed. So we were stuck there. Every time we tried to put speed on her, the ship would take off to one side and try to turn the tug around. We couldn't control it. So I decided, to heck with it, we'd stay there until the tide changed. So we sat there until it did, then got going again and took her into Vancouver.

Another ship, the *Vanlene*, was loaded with cars coming up the West Coast, I think from San Francisco, and looking for Seattle, in March 1972. It was foggy, and they hadn't had a sight or a fix of any kind for about three or four days. Instead of going in and looking, they just kept coming north. The first time they saw a light, they thought it was Tatoosh at the west end of the Strait of Juan de Fuca. So they decided to come in and head on up the strait. Wrong. That was Cape Beale they saw. Of course they ended up sitting on a rock farther up the coast of Vancouver Island inside of Barkley Sound. We were told to go over there on the *Sudbury II* and look at this. We couldn't do anything. The ship was up so high and dry that the forefoot was out of the water and the number four and five holds at the stern were under water. There was no way she was coming off.

The underwriters decided they wanted as many cars off of her as possible but no car that had been touched by salt water, even the tires. So the salvage crew went on board and opened up number one, two and three hatches. Then they cut down the goal posts and let them lie

Norwest 1 and *La Fille* tied together at dock, ca. 1940s, Vancouver, BC. The *La Fille* was later replaced by a new steel tug carrying the same name. CVA

over the side. That gave a clear run for the chopper to pick up the cars. We were sitting about a half-mile away, with a barge for the cars tied up alongside us, and we also supplied sleeping accommodation for people, showers and food. The chopper kept bringing these cars out. Some people say they were Dodge cars. I thought they were Dodge Darts, but I don't know. I think we got about 200 out on the barge.

The Coast Guard came out and set up a floating oil boom made up of hurricane fencing covered with very thick plastic, supported about a foot out of the water with Styrofoam logs tied to it. They also had a boat which was rudely called a "slick licker," a double-hulled, catamaran-type craft. Between the bows they had an endless band of terry towelling that ran through a mangle. This thing would drive into the oil (it had an engine on each hull) and the towelling would pick up the oil which would squeeze out through the mangle and be captured in an open drum. It didn't work. Luckily for them we had our booms up because the pontoons were leaking, and every now and then they'd bring this craft over to the tug and we'd pick it out of the water with our booms and let the water drain out of the pontoons so it would stay afloat. This seemed to be the beginning of the ecology program when everyone was trying out different things to combat oil spills, wondering what would work. Eventually, some years later, the *Vanlene* slipped off the rocks and disappeared.

CHAPTER 6

'The White Light Went Out'

L ife aboard a tug can be stiflingly dull—as when a storm-bound tug and boom are forced to shelter in a bay for days or weeks—or it can be extraordinarily hectic—as is the case for crews working with scows on the busy Fraser River. And as every career towboater knows, at some moments, life aboard includes moments of abject terror. If this unpredictability is the bane of the towboaters' days (try planning a wedding around seasonal westerlies!), it is also what keeps the job interesting.

La Fille on a cold winter day on the Fraser River. DM

In June 1953, **Captain Donald MacPherson** *was on the* La Fille *in Burrard Inlet:*

We received a call from our dispatcher to rush to an explosion and fire at Ioco. Our tug was the only one in the area with a monitor [water cannon], and that end of the inlet was out of the Vancouver fireboat's jurisdiction. The tanker *Argus* had had a fire break out while taking on high-octane gas. The crewmen were rescued and the chief engineer had closed the hatches and started up the emergency carbon dioxide system. The captain had steered the ship away from land after throwing a line to the tug *Sea Chief*. Then he jumped aboard the tug. The burning ship was drifting on the south side of the inlet with fire raging when we approached on the *La Fille* with our monitor spewing water. We had no foam. All the traffic was stopped along Barnet Highway. We continued for about two days while tank tops [hatches] exploded into the air and our tire bumpers along the side were smoking from the heat. We finally left it flaming but it burned itself out many hours later. I went aboard afterwards and saw that the radar in the wheelhouse was a puddle of glass and metal. Papers in the safe in the master's cabin were charcoal.

Captain Hugh Wallace, *of the Cates family, remembers how small errors can lead quickly to big problems:*

There used to be lots of driftwood floating around the harbour. The harbourmaster boat would get us to help them by towing a string of boomsticks—one boat on each end—and sweep around the harbour gathering up all the drift. Once we were on one end of the boomsticks and the harbourmaster's boat was on the other. I was throwing the line around the bitt and pulling it tight. One loop went halfway on the bitt and I pulled the line and it slipped off. I fell over backwards into the water over the propeller that was still going

around. I was still hanging onto the line. The other boat had seen me fall in but lost sight of me. They were blowing their whistle to get the attention of my skipper. I yelled at him to stop the engine but he couldn't hear me. The propeller was going around just under me and I had to keep my feet up. Finally I was able to climb back aboard the tug.

Years ago ships went into the berth on the east side of the Pacific Elevator. One day we were the line boat for a ship going into No. 1 berth. The tide was setting to the west so we stood by the end of the dock just in case the ship needed a push off of it, and more tugs were on the other side of the ship. I was on the top steering. The ship's wheel [propeller] was about half out of the water. We stood by as the ship slid past the end of the dock. I noticed my deckhand was pushing a large log away from our stern. I said, "Don't worry about that. I'll wash it away with our propeller." I put the tug in gear and gave it some

When the tanker *Argus* caught fire at loco in June 1953, the tug *La Fille* was called on to pump water on its burning hull. CMC

throttle. The wash started pushing the log away from our stern and we began moving ahead. I turned my head and saw that we were heading for the ship's wheel that was thrashing around. I went full astern but we were still moving ahead toward it. We seemed to take forever to stop. When we finally did, I looked astern of us and saw that the ship's wash had pushed us in between the dock and the ship with its propeller thrashing just ahead of our bow and the dock at our stern. I couldn't do anything but back full astern against the dock, hoping the tug would swing one way or the other. With the wheel still thrashing around, I pushed on the ship's rudder and swung our stern out from the dock, making a little room. I then backed out and turned to port. I just wanted to get out of there. The ship's propeller wash was still pushing at us. The ship was light in the water and it looked like its stern was going to break our mast off. I planned to crouch down and try not to get hit by it because I was outside on top. As we went around the ship's stern the tug luckily listed over and the mast cleared by inches. There must have been someone looking out for me that day. One of the longshoremen standing on the dock was just shaking his head.

The *Sudbury* rescues the Liberian freighter *Corinna*, January 2, 1975, towing her through mountainous waves and hurricane-force winds. SEASPAN INTERNATIONAL

Captain Ted King:

In 1965, on one stormy night on the Fraser River, a barge had broken loose from its tug and was adrift with no lights on about two miles from the mouth. A deep-sea ship came around the corner and the pilot had to choose between hitting the barge or a sandbar, so he hit the bar. That was the best way to go. The next day 15 tugs were ready at high tide to attempt to get the ship off—two pushing from the bow, two pulling at each side and the rest attached bow to stern with tow lines, pulling in two rows at the ship's stern. I assisted on the *Le Prince*. The ship slid off with no problems.

***Captain Alan Wood**, whose early career included work aboard the venerable* Master *knows the dangers of ship-docking:*

We were sent out on the *Cates XX* about 2:30 p.m. on June 21, 1974, with two other tugs to assist the *Beishu Maru*, a Japanese container ship, into Centennial Pier No. 6. The ship made one attempt and due to the strong tides couldn't get into the dock. She made a second attempt and couldn't do it. They requested that a tow line be put onto the stern of the ship and that we pull it out into the harbour for a third attempt. Which I did. On the third try we were getting very close to the dock, the attempt again starting to go a bit sour, and the pilot ordered the engine room to give him half-speed ahead. With us on the tow line at the stern, right near the propeller, a large roll of water came out and as soon as it hit the tug it immediately rolled us over. We sank. In the process my crewman, Frank Fegan, drowned. I somehow survived and came to the surface and was picked up by one of the tugs running around looking for survivors. While I was trapped under the tug, there was no sensation of water, everything was very quiet, even though there was turbulence all around. I was badly bruised and knocked around but I had no sense of that at all. I didn't know that I had been beaten up, in a sense. Everything was peaceful and quiet and out to a distance all the water had turned a very bright white, like a light. The whole area was white. The white light went out and I then knew where I was. I started to fight to get up to the surface. I was under the top deck which was above my head. The crewman that was with me was in the cabin inside. With the rushing water going in through the door, he had no chance to get out.

When I went to the coroner's inquest, the courts were going to charge me with the death of my crewman. I had to wait three years for my case to get to court. My explanation to all the lawyers of what happened proved to be true. I had told them about the big wall of water coming out and the approximate time that this engine movement order was given on the *Beishu Maru*. The lawyers sent down to Portland, Oregon, the next stop for the ship, for the engine room recorders, with the times and orders, and they were exactly the same times as I had said. I was exonerated completely of whatever happened. The pilot and the shipping company were charged with the event.

One night, about nine o'clock, I had another fairly close call. I had started off to pick a pilot up in English Bay at a nearby anchorage. We were about 1,000 feet off of Stanley Park and we hit a piece of driftwood. I stopped the engine and we waited for a "clunk" to see if it had hit the wheel or not. Nothing happened so we went on. Then I had a notion that we should go back and look at the hull. I sent the deckhand back to open the after hatch and see if everything looked all right and he shouted out, "The boat's full of water!" I thought, How could it be? I checked the hatch and sure enough it was full, so I checked to see if West Vancouver or Stanley Park was closer. I decided to go back to Stanley Park. I went slowly, and that particular part that I was heading for had a lot of rocks. I felt our way along, and we didn't hit any rocks and managed to get up to within a couple of feet of the seawall. When we were approaching it the deckhand threw the life raft over and I questioned him because we could walk to the seawall and walk home if we wanted to. He was pushing the panic button a bit.

Captain Royal Maynard:

One night I was leaving Ragged Islands, or Copeland Isles on the chart, just above Lund, with a log tow. A beautiful calm, clear night, lights burning nicely on the tow. Just before midnight I saw a boat of

some description back at the tail end of our tow, and I finally got hold of him on the radio to find out what he was doing back there. He was trying to pull a speedboat out of the boom. He had already taken two or three people out, one who had a broken arm and another who was just shook up. The speedboat had come roaring down through Thulin Passage and went right between the two tail-end lanterns on the tow. He went in a section and a half over the logs. Just another reason for not trusting pleasure boaters too much.

In 1970, I was on the *Viking King* tied to a log tow over in Lyall Harbour in the Gulf Islands. We heard on the radio about an accident in Active Pass, which was a Russian freighter [the *Sergey Yesenin*] that had sliced into the ferry *Queen of Victoria*. The bow of the ship was

Dressed up with flags, the *Viking King* parades at Expo 86 in False Creek. The tug was later sold to a private owner and used as a yacht, 1986. DM

over halfway into the ferry. We ran up there to see if we could be of assistance. They drifted out into the Gulf of Georgia. There were literally hundreds of boats around and two or three other ferries. It was a terrible thing to see. They tried to separate the two vessels and the Russian ship went full astern and the ferry went sideways with him. They were jammed in that tight. Finally, the *Haida Brave*, which later became the *Commodore Straits*, about a 130-foot tug with 3,700 hp and the *Queen*, one of Rivtow's boats, got up against the ferry and started pushing on it and the deep-sea ship went astern and that did separate them. I remember the anchor of the deep-sea ship dragging across the passenger deck up top, pulling out handrails and that. There were three people killed in that accident—a mother and baby who were down on the car deck and another fellow down there who was also killed. One thing I could not understand about that accident was they did not remove the passengers off the ferry before they separated the two vessels. To me that has always seemed such a chance because you still don't know what's going to happen when they're separated.

Captain Ron Westmoreland *saw mishaps from the point of view of a captain and a dispatcher:*

When my employer L & K Lumber's yard was on fire in North Vancouver, we wanted the Vancouver fireboat to come in to the front of the mill. That would be the best spot; give it a shot of water and they could have put the fire out. It was right around four or five o'clock in the afternoon. We couldn't get the use of the Vancouver fireboat for North Van unless the mayor of Vancouver gave his permission. He was on his way home. So we had to wait an hour or so until they reached him. It was too late. They just came over in time to knock the mill down with a big water monitor. Then some years later while I was dispatching, a yacht caught fire in Coal Harbour. The fireboat at the time

was in the shipyard for repairs. They had a replacement fireboat and it wouldn't start. It was quite cold out. The fire chief commandeered the *Jean L.* which happened to be over in the area. It towed that burning boat out to where the Nine O'Clock Gun is, at Stanley Park, and he used his own monitor to try and douse the flames, which is pretty hard to do with a fibreglass boat. It finally sank, which was great. The fire was out and he buoyed the yacht with a nylon tow line and a brand new life jacket until such time as it could be lifted for investigation. We didn't charge for that service. When it came time to lift the boat our tow line and life jacket had mysteriously disappeared. Nobody knew anything about it. I was rather disturbed about that, just the principle of it. So I sent a bill off to Vancouver city hall with a full explanation about what happened. Some clerk there got all up in the air about it and phoned Mr. Lyttle, the owner of our company, and attempted to embarrass him by explaining our civic duty, and so on. Mr. Lyttle came

Tugs *Chemainus*, *Robert Preston* and *Sea Lion* at the dock in Vancouver, May 20, 1926. VMM

to me and I reminded him about the old mill fire, which he knew about, and he said to phone the guy back, which I did, and explained to him about the fire at the mill and that we couldn't get the fireboat. We didn't mind them commandeering our boat but we didn't expect to bear the cost of the tow line and life jacket. He was still a bit arrogant about it. So I said I was going to contact the newspaper about it and write to the mayor and council. He just about broke into tears and he went to see Mr. Lyttle and begged him to stop me because he could lose his job. I wanted him to know that it's a two-way street and these clerks don't always know what's happened in the past. We got paid. He sent over a cheque by courier.

Captain Adrian Bull, *who helped salvage the barge* Forest Prince *from Long Beach:*

The mill at Squamish blew its boiler, so Island Tug got the job of running black and green liquor from Grays Harbor [Wash.] to Squamish. It's something used for bleaching paper—very caustic. They used the old log barges, the *Island Pine, Island Hemlock, Island Spruce,* to take this stuff down and back. I was on the *Sudbury* as second mate and as we got out with this barge off Neah Bay it broke in two. The ends came up and kissed. The stern then went down but the bow would not sink. We had to tow it in off Becher Bay and Jack Daly, the diver, came out and put a charge in it and sank it. The *Sudbury II* had another barge, same business. She managed to make it out around Tatoosh and the same thing, down again. Only she lost both pieces. The liquor dissipated in salt water.

Captain Larry Baese:

I remember I was still decking and we were heading up north with mate Cecil Haycock. It was the first trip north for me. I'd never been up there because we had been towing logs from Centre Bay and Long Bay on Howe Sound to the river and False Creek and the harbour for months and months and it was getting boring, as well as being really hard work. We'd take two tows to the river and one to Burrard Inlet, then we'd get 24 hours off. We'd get back on board and were more tired then than when we got off. So we were really happy about going up north. One night about one or two o'clock, Cecil was on watch. He turned the light on in the wheelhouse to read the tide book or something and he put us right up on Ragged Islands. He saw the island just before he hit it, and he rang "Stop" on the bells and jingles, and "Full Astern." The second engineer didn't understand the bells. He felt it sounded like "Stop Engine" and "Full Ahead." He got "Stop" and "Full Ahead," which was the signal from the wheelhouse to "Come and give me a cup of coffee." He started up the ladder to go to the wheelhouse when all of a sudden, "Bang, bang, bang." Not that it would have helped even if he had stopped the engines because we were so close to the island we would have hit it anyway. Maybe we wouldn't have gone quite as far as the trees. There were a couple of tugs tied up for weather at Ragged Islands with log tows and they came and stood by us in case the tug didn't lift when the tide came in. We were there for 12 hours on the rocks. This little boat, *Coyle No. 3*, was really good because once

The barge *Island Maple*, in tow of the *Sudbury*, broke up and sank in high seas off Cape Flattery, October 1963.
SEASPAN INTERNATIONAL

the tide came in she just floated herself off and we carried on.

It was in the late '70s and we were running a tow with the *R.B. Green* out of Seymour Inlet, just coming down through Schooner Pass. I noticed the boat was really sluggish to steer. I sent the deckhand down to the engine room to have a look around, and he came back and told me everything was fine. The weather was really sour that day, so I thought rather than taking the tow as far as Southgates, I would take it into Allison Harbour and tie up in there because I didn't like the way the boat felt. And just before we got into the tie-up spot, I ran down to the engine room to have a look myself, and here the boat was full of water. The coupling was catching the water and throwing it all around the engine room. I got into Allison Harbour and tied up at the first spot I could. I went down to the engine room and started to try and get this thing pumped out. We had three automatic bilge pumps all in a line from the deepest to the highest, and for some reason they weren't working. I fired up the auxiliary to get the large bilge pump to start pumping. As a rule it ran well but I couldn't make the pumps work. So we got really excited. The water was already over the floorboards in the stern of the engine room. When a boat gets heavy in the water it sinks below the water-line and often it leaks more because the wood is so dry there. I told my son to go up on the top deck and start the large gas-fired scow pump and get the radios ready because we were probably going to have to holler a mayday, since there was no way we could stop this water from coming in. As a last resort, for some reason, I tried the auxiliary one more time, and it started to suck water. Once we got it pumped out, the crew was all happy and ready to go out and have supper. I said no, we had to find out why this thing wouldn't pump because we wouldn't want to do this again in the middle of the night. With the auxiliary shut off we pulled all the deck plates off and checked the lines. We found a rust pocket on one of the pipes. All the water was running out of our bilge line. I used a trick that George Brown, an old engineer, showed me. I took an old piece of the coupling hose and cut it in half, slid it over the end of the pipe and filled it full of grease. Then we put hose clamps from one end to the other, real tight. That stopped the water. We managed to get our tows home and get the tug into a shipyard and had

all new piping put in. That was a really scary time. I thought we had lost her. The weather was so bad it would have been hard for us to be rescued because Allison Harbour is at the entrance to Queen Charlotte Sound, and it was so rough out there that any rescue boat wouldn't have been able to get near enough.

Captain Joe Quilty *was on the* J.S. Foley *towing a barge of logs from Kyuquot Sound down the west coast heading for Victoria some time in the 1960s when he nearly lost his life:*

One morning I got knocked overboard when a tow line hit me. It was shortly after I started working with Kingcome Navigation. I was second mate and had gotten up in the morning to go on watch at six o'clock. Before I went up to the wheelhouse I went aft to look at the tow line because we'd had a really wild night off Nootka Sound. I noticed that the tow line had gotten out of the rollers, upright pins that kept the line centred, and they were both lying on the deck. So I went

Capt. Larry Baese's first job in 1946 was aboard the *Coyle No. 3*, a stalwart steam tug in Pacific Coyle Navigation's fleet. VMM

up to the wheelhouse and told the skipper, and he said the deckhand and I should go aft and put them back in place. So we went back and the other guy put the roller in one side and I put the second one in the other side. Then I noticed that the nut was missing off of the pin on my side, so I bent down to pick it up and an extra heavy swell came along and the tow line lifted, came out of the pin and hit me. Just knocked me over the side. It broke my hip. So there I was in the water, it was dark and the water was really rough. As soon as the skipper saw me go over the side he tossed a life ring overboard with a flare and smoke signal on it. That's how they found me. I tried to reach it but I couldn't swim because my hip was broken. I could just keep myself afloat with my arms. How the skipper did it, I'll never know. He turned around and came back and put the tug right alongside of me. They lowered a really long wooden ladder over the side and hollered at me to grab a hold of the rungs, which I did. They just tipped the ladder up and slid me out. After they put me in my cabin, the skipper came down to see me. He was as white as a sheet. That skipper, Ralph Smith, sure did a job. After they got me aboard they took me into Nootka Sound and the Air Sea Rescue had a helicopter down at Tofino at the time so they picked me up and flew me to the hospital at Tofino. I was off for about a month.

***Captain Cliff Julseth**'s expertise was the Fraser River:*

Spring freshets can always be a problem on the Fraser River but the one in 1948 was exceptional. The winter weather of 1947 – 48 held off through January and half of February while I was still logging. When the snow pack came it seemed to snow forever. By the first of March it was evident that we weren't going to be doing any logging because of the snow, so that prompted me to go on the tugs. For six weeks we didn't do any log towing because there just wasn't enough water in the river. When it did start to rise, we started towing. The water never stopped rising but we kept on towing until

Opposite: The *La Fille* tows the historic steam tug SS *Master* to a temporary berth in False Creek. Vancouver's Burrard Bridge is in the background. DM

Capt. Cliff Julseth, ca. 1986.

it became unsafe. If we had lost control of a log tow it would have floated right through Chilliwack. So then we switched to what you might call salvage—with people, cattle, feed, food—taking them from the low lands to the high lands, you might say.

During that period, Hope always held what they called Brigade Days. One of the events was the Indian war canoe races. As a safety precaution, we brought the tugs from Bristol Island out to be there in case of capsize, to pick anybody out of the water. When we arrived and put the bows against the beach, I jumped off and poked a stick into the sand at the edge of the water as a mark. The water was rising an inch an hour in that area. The weather was fiercely hot. From then until June 15 or so was the really serious hazard period of the '48 flood. The water was 24½ feet on the gauge at Mission. Several of the existing dikes broke through. There have been times since that the water has gotten very close to that level but in the meantime they have built up a new dike system, so we haven't had the same problems.

A lot of the islands along the Fraser had a big population of people who normally wouldn't have to move. But under the circumstances they had to get off and move to higher ground. The people went first on a landing craft but with the tugs we tried to get the animals out—the cows and pigs and chickens, and all the grain, etc. The village of Agassiz pretty well vacated and the residents moved up onto the hill into the graveyard area and camped out. The cows had to be milked and they couldn't give the milk away because of the water, so they just milked them onto the ground.

The debris coming down the river during that flood was just amazing. There were dead animals, lumber, logs, brush, trees, you name it. It was piling up everywhere. We had one boom of logs, five sections, that had been tied to a tree at the river's edge. The water went over the river's banks, the boom swung on the wire that was tied to a tree and ended up in the middle of a farmer's pasture. When the water went down, it was still intact and had to be removed with tractors, moved to the water, then put back into the water after it went down.

Most of the old-time Fraser River skippers remember the incident in 1947 when the tug Red Fir 5 *broke down with engine problems on the Fraser south of Hope. It was captured by the* Red Fir 6 *to be towed and it had engine problems, too. So the two of them, side by side, drifted down the river to the top of a log-jam pile sitting on top of a gravel bar. The current forced both of them under and they sank. There was really no place deep enough to sink. They just rolled over and went under the logs and jammed there. The crew was able to get off onto the pile with some food but they had to sit there and wait for rescue. They tried to heat a can of spaghetti on a fire but the can exploded, sending spaghetti all over the place. Old-timers still call that spot Spaghetti Point, even though the actual bar has washed away.*

Captain Cliff Julseth:

In 1946 or '47 on the Fraser River north of Mission, one of the skippers and his deckhand noticed a black head moving along in the river near the tug, small black nose leading. The bears always look smaller in the water than they actually are, so the skipper moved the tug closer and the deckhand make a loop in the bow mooring line that was fixed to a bollard, and as the tug got beside the bear, dropped the loop over its head. The tug moved astern to tighten the loop. As you can imagine, the bear became very agitated and when he was washed against the tug's side, reached up with his paws and clawed his way up onto the tug's forward deck. The men were shocked to see the size of it, figuring that it weighed about 450 pounds, more than they could handle. The deckhand made a beeline for the wheelhouse with the bear close behind. Fortunately the line was still looped tightly around his neck and he was pulled up short, clawing at the wheelhouse window. The tight line kept his paws about six inches away from the glass. While he was lunging at the window, he caught his hind feet on the hatch cover, which he proceeded to tear up and throw overboard. Just under that hatch was the fo'c'sle where the deckhand's bunk was located. He was a pretty smart dresser and had a new suit hanging up just under the hatch. The bear reached down, grabbed the suit and tore it up into about seven pieces. At this the deckhand grabbed the fire axe and went outside to try and cut the line but couldn't reach it without getting too close to the raging bear. So the skipper, who all this time was watching speechless, began swinging the wheel from side to side, slewing the boat back and forth. The bear slid off the deck into the water and when the line slackened, it slid off of his neck. No more bear catching for that crew.

Biographies

Captain Cyril Andrews began his career on the CPR ship *Princess Charlotte* in 1929, then worked almost continuously on tugs until 1945 when injury forced him ashore. He was instrumental in starting the first search and rescue service on the coast. At age 89 he would sit in his favourite armchair, cane between his knees, binoculars nearby for checking out vessels in Burrard Inlet and a VHF 10-channel radio scanner near at hand. Captain Andrews died in May 2003.

Captain Larry Baese went to work as a novice deckhand in January 1946. After five years with Pacific Coyle Navigation, Captain Baese moved to the Fraser River-based Burt and Reid Towing, and later Towers Towing on Sea Island and Stradiotti Brothers. He received his master's ticket March 18, 1954, and captained Stradiotti's *Strady 7*. He also worked for Amos Beckman, Pacific Pine Lumber Company, and for some years at Rivtow Marine and Great West Towing & Salvage. On January 6, 1975, Captain Baese bought the 65-foot tug, *R.B. Green*. His company, Dollar Navigation Limited, towed logs out of Lake Bay and Hole in the Wall, Seymour, Toba, and Bute Inlets. Captain Baese retired in 1990.

Captain Adrian Bull started his career at sea in January 1949 on British ships. He received his British Foreign-going Licence (Master F/G) for deep-sea vessels and travelled around the world twice. He joined Island Tug & Barge Limited in 1962, where he served as deckhand for one year and skipper for eight years. He came ashore in 1972, worked for Yarrows Shipbuilding in Victoria, then for Hess Oil in St. Croix, the Virgin Islands, until August 1995 when he returned to Vancouver Island.

Captain Bull comments: "I would like to say thank you to all the guys who sailed with me on *Sudbury II*. They were a great bunch and helped me make it look easy. A lot of names have disappeared from my memory bank but I remember Jimmy Talbot and Harry Tebbs, Bob Gray and George Winterburn, Brick Metson, Norm Bourne, Leendert Van Neck, John Kendall, Gerry Gaudette and a pastry chef/cook who could produce three trays of different fancies before breakfast without breaking a sweat. These are a few of the guys who made it all work. Thank you, all, I do miss the old days."

Captain Aage (Buster) Fransvaag was born in Trondheim, Norway and went to sea at the age of 17 on a Norwegian three-masted barque cadet ship. His first sight of Canadian tugs was about 1948 from high on the deck of a Norwegian freighter in Burrard Inlet. He worked for six and a half years for Gulf of Georgia Towing Company as a deckhand and mate, then joined Vancouver Tugboat Company based in Coal Harbour as a skipper in 1969. He retired in 1993.

John Henderson started as a deckhand on the *Masset* in the early 1930s. Shortly afterwards he went to sea on an Imperial Oil tanker, then served in the Canadian Navy from 1940 until the end of the war. In 1949 he became an engineer on the

S.D. Brooks of Kingcome Navigation, then worked for M.R. Cliff Tugboat Company on the *Sea Swell*, *Moresby* and *Haro*, all steam tugs. He worked on various large ships for 12 years in the 1950s and early 1960s. After acting as third engineer on the Alaska cruise ship TSS (Twin-Screw Steamer) *Prince George*, then on the *Wm. J. Stewart*, he retired in 1979.

Captain Clifford Julseth started in March 1948 with River Towing Company (later Rivtow Marine) for Silver Skagit Logging Company as mate on a small, shallow draft tug. Based at Hope, his tug towed log booms down the Fraser River to the mouth of the Vedder Canal and also in Harrison Lake. He earned his master's ticket in 1955 and moved to the office as dispatcher in 1956. Becoming manager three years later, he moved on to vice-president of marine operations in 1980. Captain Julseth retired in 1990 after 42 years with River Towing, Rivtow Marine and Rivtow Straits Limited.

Captain Howie Keast started at C.H. Cates & Sons as a deckhand in 1939 at the age of 17. He joined Escott Towing on Burrard Inlet three and a half years later and stayed for 14 years. He then joined Lyttle Brothers (later North Arm Transportation), where he remained for 30 years.

Captain A.E. (Ted) King grew up in Steveston, bought his first fish boat at age 16, and fished the Fraser River and Rivers Inlet. He started at Vancouver Tugboat Company in 1964 as deckhand on the harbour tugs for the first year then moved to the Fraser River. He received his master's papers November 21, 1969 and took over the *La Bette*. He worked in Vancouver harbour until 1976, skippering the *La Mite*, *Seaspan Trojan* and others, then worked dispatch until 1980 when he went back on river tugs. From 1989 until the present he has been a Fraser River pilot.

Captain Robert (Bob) McCoy first went to sea in 1944 as deckboy on the *Princess Alice* and the next year worked on his first tug, the *Strath*, of Victoria Tugboats, as oiler and deckhand. For the next few years he travelled the world on deep-water ships and on coastal freighters. In July 1962, he started work for Straits Towing on the *Magellan Straits* and worked on several other Straits tugs. He received his master's ticket in 1964. His first job as mate was on the *Canso Straits*. Over the years he has worked for Canadian Tugboat Company, Coast Ferries, Vancouver Tugboat Company, Northland Navigation, Gulf of Georgia Towing Company and Seaspan International. He also worked one season in the Arctic with NTCL. He retired from the tugboat industry in 1995. He presently works as master for Harbour Cruises in Burrard Inlet.

Captain Donald MacPherson came from Ontario to Ocean Falls when he was 18. His first job on a tug was in 1951 as deckhand on the *La Dene* of Vancouver Tugboat Company, towing logs from Bella Coola to Ocean Falls and paper barges from Ocean Falls to Vancouver. He received his master's ticket in 1958 and became skipper of the *La Mite*. He worked on Burrard Inlet and the Fraser River setting up tows for outside tugs, serving sawmills in False Creek, the harbour and the river. After skippering several Vancouver Tug vessels, he moved to the new *Seaspan Discovery* in March 1984 and also the *Seaspan Guardian* as skipper. He worked 42 years for Seaspan International and retired in 1993.

Captain Royal Maynard started as a deckhand at the age of 17 in 1960 and got his master's ticket in 1966. He worked for Swiftsure Towing, Stradiotti Brothers (North Arm Transportation) and for the last 35 years, Rivtow Marine. His hauls have included log booms, freight, oil, and gravel barges. For the past number of years he has skippered the *Rivtow Capt. Bob*.

Captain Joe Quilty received his master's ticket in 1940 and became quartermaster on the *Princess Victoria* and several other CPR ships. He joined the army in 1941 and was mate (and later skipper) on the target-towing tug *General Lake*. After the war he worked for Stone Brothers, then skippered the pilot boat out of Port Alberni to Bamfield and Cape Beale. He also worked for Kingcome Navigation, BC Ferries and the Department of Fisheries. Captain Quilty retired in 1982.

Captain Alan Stanley spent his childhood on Quadra Island and from age 10 fished with his father at Rivers Inlet. At 13, on his summer holidays, he worked as second engineer on the *Harris No. 8* of Pacific Coyle Navigation and saw first-hand the miserable conditions firemen and coal passers worked in. By 15 he was working as a deckhand on Coyle's *Peerless*. In 1948 he became deckhand on the *Norshore* and continued as mate until 1952 when he moved to Vancouver Tugboat Company. He received his master's certificate in 1955; the *La Rose* was his first command. On the *La Rose* and other tugs, he towed chip, hog fuel, and gravel scows from Vancouver to Howe Sound, Vancouver Island and elsewhere. Captain Stanley stayed with Van Tug until he became a BC Coast Pilot in 1967. He retired in 1997.

Captain Hugh Wallace started working part time at C.H. Cates & Sons in 1959 at the age of 15. Later he worked full time as a deckhand and in the company shop. He received his master's ticket in 1972 and began running Cates tugs. His first task as a skipper was to tow a ship to Saskatchewan Wheat Pool on Burrard Inlet. Since that time he has skippered several Cates tugs. After tractor tugs were introduced, he started on the *Cates II*. He has worked out of Deltaport on the *Seaspan Hawk* but has spent most of his career in the harbour at Burrard Inlet. Captain Wallace

is a grandson of towboating pioneer Charles Henry Cates.

Captain Ron Westmoreland was 15 when he began working weekends at C.H. Cates & Sons in 1944. In 1949 he moved to L & K Lumber, working on the *Marjorie L.* as deckhand, towing logs and lumber barges, or shunting booms in the booming grounds. He received his master's certificate in 1957, taking over as master on the *Jean L.*. About 1965 he came ashore to work as dispatcher for L & K and stayed until they went into bankruptcy in 1986, when he moved to North Arm Transportation and later, Noble Towing. In 1991 he left towboating but three sons and a daughter-in-law carry on the tradition.

Captain Westmoreland emphasizes that the praise he received from companies for dispatching jobs well done belongs to the men on the tugs; he believes they were some of the best in the business, especially harbour skippers Iven Northcott, Dave Cannon, Roy Spicer, Walt Rankin, Don Westmoreland and Bob Cannon.

Captain Alan Wood started as a dishwasher on Union Steamship's the *Camosun* in 1945. He then worked as a deckhand on the tugs *Chilliwack* and *Island King* of Frank Waterhouse Company. He was deckhand on the *RFM* of Marpole Towing Company with his uncle, Harry Jones, and was also on the *Master* and the *Marpole*. He joined Young and Gore on the *Sea Lion*, towing logs from Seymour Inlet to Long Bay in Howe Sound. He then moved to M.R. Cliff Tugboat Company and Vancouver Tugboat Company in Coal Harbour. He received his master's papers in 1953. Captain Wood was with C.H. Cates & Sons from 1969 until he retired in 1995.

Glossary

bag booms—a corral of boomsticks chained together to contain driftwood or logs. Sometimes two tugs will pull a U-shaped bag boom to clear an area of debris.

beachcomber—a.) a durable, usually aluminum or steel-hulled boat that locates and gathers loose logs; b.) a person who makes all or part of their income by salvaging logs; c.) when a towboat takes its tow close to shore, looking for favourable current

bight—the loop of rope or cable as distinguished from the ends. In towboating, as in logging, the bight is a dangerous place, hence the commonly heard advice to novices, "Keep out of the bight."

bitts—a pair of strong posts projecting above a boat or ship's deck, used for securing wire or rope lines; also mounted on the gunwales of some vessels

boomboats (or dozers)—small, powerful and manoeuvrable boats that move logs or booms into position

boomsticks—logs, usually 66 feet long, with a hole drilled in either end. Boomsticks are connected with boomchains to enclose the perimeter of a log boom.

bridles—wire rope or chain, usually with an eye in each end, used for towing barges or logs to give equal pull on each side and

make the barges tow in a straight line

bulwarks—a solid structure extending above the level of a main deck for the protection of persons or objects on deck

bundles—logs bound with cables to form bundles. Bundle booms are more seaworthy than flat booms.

cabbage patch—the area at Powell River on Grief Point, the location of a former cabbage garden

cutting doughnuts—said of a tug and tow doing large circles while awaiting tides or weather

dodger—a barrier, sometimes made of canvas, that protects the walkway in front of the wheelhouse windows or anywhere on board as a shelter from wind

dogs—pointed pieces of metal with a hole in one end that are pounded or screwed into logs at the ends of the booms; then doglines are threaded through them and secured to keep the logs from escaping in heavy seas. Dogs that are screwed into the logs were known as Oregon dogs and were used on tows that had to cross stretches of open water, i.e. towing out across the Nitinat bar and down Juan de Fuca Strait.

fluorescence—actually bioluminescence, it is caused by tiny deep-water creatures that

come near the water surface in the dark and shine

goalposts—two Sampson or king posts often joined at the top with a catwalk, with the main mast continuing up from the top of the catwalk

guthammer—an old term referring to the dinner gong, usually a triangle

houseworks—a room on top of the boat, may contain the wheelhouse

jungle—the island- and channel-strewn area north of Yuculta Rapids and the Seymour Narrows

knot—1.15 miles per hour

Kort nozzle—a non-steering nozzle with a rudder behind it. The Kort nozzle differs from nozzles that can turn and steer the boat

log towing straps—heavy wire rope straps that are shackled, choked or figure-eighted around the side sticks near the head end of the booms and are then shackled into the towing bridles

mast lights—one light means that the vessel is running light, two vertical lights mean the tug has a tow, three vertical lights warn that the tug has a tow over 600 feet in length

monkey's fist—the knot shaped like a ball on the throwing end of a heaving line

monkey island—the controls on the uppermost deck above the wheelhouse

outflow wind—wind coming from the land. In winter on the BC coast, outflow winds are often associated with icy temperatures

outside—working a tug outside of protected water; the Strait of Georgia, or up the coast, for example

paper scows—specially built barges with enclosed waterproof storage areas for moving paper products such as newsprint

peavey—a sturdy, 1.5-metre long, sharp-pointed pole with a hook near one end, used for rolling logs

pennant (or pendant)—a length of wire, shackled into towing bridles, part of the towing gear on a tug and used to connect barges; enables the tug's crew to unshackle and work on the tow when necessary

pike pole—a lightweight 4-5-metre long aluminum pole, tipped with a steel point. Essential equipment for deckhands used to reach submerged tie-up lines and boom chains, or to move loose logs.

pitch of the propeller—how far ahead the boat is pushed in one revolution of the propeller (eg. 12-inch pitch, the boat moves ahead 12 feet in one revolution)

pulling full—towing at full power

pulling light—pulling an empty barge or scow

pylons—pillars at the end of a log barge that act as log stops, also as a safe retreat for crew when the barge is tipping off logs

riders—the first and last swifter in a tow

running easy—running about three-quarters speed

running light—moving ahead with no tow

Sampson braid—two lines in one, separated from each other, an inner core and an outer rope

sea anchor—often a canvas bag, cone-shaped and open at both ends, dropped forward off a vessel at the end of a cable to hold the bow into the wind or sea during a storm; some used to have vegetable oil attached near the anchor to smooth down the seas

smoke pit—engine room

southeast wires—light wires that are choked around the side stick at the outside forward edge of the tow and then wrapped or figure-eighted around several of the outside logs to make the forward corners of the tow able to withstand more weather

sticks—see boomsticks

swifter—one or more logs attached across the middle of a flat boom to hold the boomsticks in position

tag line—a line about 300 feet long attached to a floating buoy at a barge's stern and a cable along the length of the barge that can be used to retrieve it if the tug's tow line breaks

thimble—a metal ring with a concave groove on the outside, used to line a ring of rope, forming an eye

tow line—long wires on a winch at the after end of the tug, their diameter determined by the tug's size and horsepower. Most coastal tugs have two pennants in their tow lines and the links on them are made of strong alloyed steel, the links having a hole in them to enable bridles to be shackled in for tandem towing.

'tween straps—wire straps about nine feet long that were put in every second or third section down the inside strings of a log tow to hold it together

waiting weather—waiting in a sheltered location until the heavy weather eases

waiting tide—waiting until the tide is favourable to continue

wheel—the steering wheel of the tug, or its propeller

winch—large powered drum usually mounted at the after end of the tug's houseworks. The amount of line between the tug and the tow is controlled by a winch brake.

wires—steel cables up to two and a half inches in diameter used as tow lines

Index